The ELECTRONIC Campus

A Case History of the First Comprehensive High-access Academic Computing Network at a Public University

By Jon T. Rickman & Dean L. Hubbard

PRESCOTT PUBLISHING CO.

P.O. Box. 713, Maryville, MO 64468

Printed in the United States of America
1st Edition: August 1992
10 9 8 7 6 5 4 3 2 1

ISBN 0-9633819-9-7

Library of Congress Catalog Card Number: 92-93868

Designed and Edited by Carole Gieseke

TABLE OF CONTENTS

SECTION TWO: OPERATING THE SYSTEM

SECTION THREE: SECURING THE FUTURE

SECTION FOUR: APPENDIX

FOREWORD

A fascinating poster entitled "Man's Best Friends" hangs on the wall of AASCU's headquarters. Depicted is a college student sitting at a computer terminal in a residence hall room with a dog at his side. A sub-caption advises, "Dog Not Included." The poster promotes Northwest Missouri State University's Electronic Campus, an innovative system of computers which networks every office and residence hall room on campus with each other. It also networks these offices and rooms with an incredible array of databases and software applications. Whether or not we're ready to assign equal "friend" status to our computers as we historically have done with "Fido," hardly anyone can challenge the assertion that in our technologically-based society a working knowledge of computers is essential. College and university officials understand this challenge and struggle to find ways of providing the hardware, instruction and experience necessary so that tomorrow's graduates are competent in this rapidly evolving field.

For this reason, *The Electronic Campus* is particularly timely. It describes a system which is at once comprehensive, technologically doable, educationally effective, and affordable. This is quite an accomplishment. President Hubbard originally convinced the Missouri legislature to fund the system as a "low cost alternative for public institutions" where 75 percent of the students cannot afford to purchase or choose not to purchase an expensive microcomputer such as is currently being required by a few private institutions. Even though, in the high-priced world of computers, the system has proven to be remarkably inexpensive to install and maintain, breadth and depth of exposure have not been compromised in order to hold down costs. Not only can students access a host of software applications and databases from their own rooms, they can work on highly restricted applications in 15 microcomputer laboratories scattered across campus, each of which is dedicated to some specialized task (e.g., desk-top publishing).

It is this carefully managed balance between comprehensive access and specialized need that may be the most unique feature of the Electronic Campus. The system stands on the principle that equipment should be acquired based on needs, not wants. Also, it reflects the insight that while students share many common computing needs all through their college careers (e.g., word processing), as they progress in their field of specialization their computing needs become more focused and, therefore, they will need access to a diverse array of hardware and software.

Certainly the institutions making up the American Association of State Colleges and Universities (AASCU) will want to give close attention to this book. While every college or university has its own unique set of circumstances and needs, much can be learned from the experience of Northwest Missouri State University when it comes to computing, particularly as it impacts undergraduate students.

Following a visit to Northwest Missouri State University to deliver a speech on political journalism in 1989, the well-known ABC newscaster Brit Hume (a computer expert himself) wrote a nationally syndicated column on the Electronic Campus. He concluded with this observation: “Parents paying five times as much to send their kids to colleges that also require them to buy computers can only wonder why other institutions haven't installed similar. . . systems. As word of what's happening [at Northwest] spreads, more seem likely to do so.” I second his observation.

James B. Appleberry
President
American Association of Colleges and Universities

PREFACE

For over 30 years higher education has sought to keep pace with the expanding role of computers in American society. It has not been easy. First of all, computers are expensive to install, service and operate. Second, computer technology has evolved at a dizzying tempo with each new generation eclipsing the previous one. Third, since learning to use a computer necessitates the mastering of rather complex and very unforgiving protocols, learners need continuous ready access to a computer and frequent practice before it can be said that they are "computer proficient."

Northwest Missouri State University in Maryville has taken several dramatic steps designed to meet these challenges and prepare its students for the emerging information-driven, technology-based society. These have included equipping every faculty office and student residence hall room with a data line, a computer terminal, and a telephone line to access sophisticated electronic applications. In addition, each residence hall room is equipped with a cable television connection to a University-owned channel dedicated to user-controlled direct-access instruction. All three of these components are networked through the University's timesharing computers. The result is an Electronic Campus made up of 2,300 terminals, a similar number of telephones with both electronic text and personal voice mailboxes, plus 500 microcomputers and powerful workstations. All of the 32-bit computers and microcomputers are connected over a high speed fiber optics network with a channel capacity of 10.5 million bits per second.

Since the system was installed in 1987, there has been an increasing interest in what Northwest has done. In addition to being featured in several publications, ABC's Brit Hume wrote a syndicated column describing the effects of the system which appeared in most of the nation's major newspapers. Later, the Associated Press distributed a lengthy article by Amanda Davis which appeared in newspapers across the nation and in the electronic publication, *PRODIGY*, an on-line computer-based news service. Most recently, *USA Today* (December 19, 1990), in a special section on computers in elementary, secondary and higher education, selected Northwest as its example of a post-secondary institution on the "high-tech cutting edge." Visitors from institutions in the United States and abroad have journeyed to Maryville to view the system first hand.

Several elements distinguish Northwest's system. First, it is extensive. Every student room, faculty and administrative office is connected. Second, it is comprehensive. In addition to providing easy access to hundreds of computing applications via terminals or microcomputers, the system includes educational video options available through two University-operated cable television channels and a telephone voice response system which utilizes computer-generated voice equipment. For example, in a single evening, a student might (1) access the library, (2) use word processing or some other software application to complete a class assignment, (3) view an instructional video on TV, (4) check their voice mail box, (5) communicate with a classmate via E-mail, (6) check on class openings and closings, (7) preregister for the next semester, and (8) access a CRAY supercomputer via a Wide Area Network in a neighboring state – all without leaving his or her residence hall room.

Third, and to some the most interesting feature of Northwest's Electronic Campus, the system is built around a cluster of VAX timesharing computers. In actuality, Northwest's approach has two components: (1) a powerful timesharing system used for processing applications of interest to large numbers of the campus community; augmented by (2), a smaller number of microcomputers and computer workstations for the specialized needs of small numbers of faculty and advanced students.

Even though this approach is contrary to recent prevailing wisdom which suggests that everything must be done on a microcomputer, or on microcomputers connected via Local Area Networks, after installing and gaining experience in supporting both types of networks, we believe that Northwest's Electronic Campus is the most effective resource allocation and least expensive approach, certainly for the small- or medium-sized college or university. A related and equally important perspective adopted by Northwest is that computing should be viewed as a utility: an adequate service supplied with the focus on tasks to be accomplished, not hardware. Both of these concepts are developed in the chapters that follow.

The system has now been operating for more than five years and has clearly moved beyond the adventure stage. Extensive data have been collected on millions of student and faculty sessions, as well as on operating costs and efforts required to keep the system current. Thus, this book has been written to share Northwest's experience and insights with other institutions struggling to find a cost-effective way to attenuate, if not completely satisfy, their students' and faculties' insatiable appetite for computing resources.

The book is divided into three sections. The first section traces the history of computing at Northwest in the context of the institution's "gestalt;" that is, its size, the nature of its faculty and student body, and the degree programs offered. Even though the assessment of ultimate impact is as difficult with computing as it is with any other aspect of education, we conclude the first section by broaching, if not exhausting, the "so what?" question. Hopefully, adequate benchmarks for comparison are provided throughout for other institutions as they contemplate which strategy would be most appropriate in their unique setting. This section is written with presidents and chief academic, student and financial officers in mind.

The second section of the book describes in technical terms exactly how the Northwest Electronic Campus is configured. This section also presents the successful strategies employed in implementing, operating and maintaining such an extensive complex of technology. Obviously, this section will be of particular interest to computing services directors and faculty who teach in related fields.

In the final section we briefly try our hand at soothsaying. (Why not? People with far less to go on than we have do it!) What is likely to happen in the near and distant future in computing and what do possible developments portend for colleges and universities? This section should appeal to all of those forced to make policy decisions in this area since it concludes by developing an agenda of issues that need to be resolved before an institution embarks on an effort to computerize its campus.

While we obviously are enthusiastic about the efforts completed to date at Northwest, we have tried to conscientiously and meticulously catalog the problems along with the successes encountered over the last five years.

Before acknowledging our debts, a word about words seems appropriate. Computing is a rapidly evolving field: It has only been 30 years since computers began to appear outside of the research labs on campuses and only 20 years since the introduction of the Scelbi 8-H, the first microcomputer. During this period, a lot of words have been invented or appropriated to describe this revolutionary device. In some instances trade names have been given a generic application (not unlike what happened with the terms "Kleenex" and "Xerox"). As a result, sometimes two terms are used to describe the same thing as in the case of "microcomputer" and "PC" (PC and Personal Computer were originally terms created by IBM in 1981). To complicate matters even more, terms that seemed precise in the beginning have become blurred in the face of technological changes. (What is a mini-computer? How does it differ from a microcomputer?) While we are sensitive to the fact that one person's jargon is another person's precision, in the interest of communicating with the largest possible audience we have arbitrarily settled on the following definitions:

"Terminal" is used to refer to a device which serves primarily as a mechanism for accessing a remote processor. Some terminals are configured so that a printer can be attached and/or graphics processed. Terminals do not contain an internal operating system or disk drives.

"Notebook computer" is used to refer to a device which has an internal operating system, can be battery operated, and weighs less than 10 pounds.

"Microcomputer" is used to refer to a desk-top computer, or PC, which has an internal central processing unit and operating system, usually require an external power supply, and which is less easily transported.

"Computer workstation" is used to refer to a very powerful microcomputer, usually having a 32 or 64 bit word length with large main memory and disk memory, plus a high resolution graphics display dedicated to a single user.

"Computing station" is coined in this book to refer to either a notebook computer, microcomputer, computer workstation or a terminal connected to a timesharing computer or computing network.

"Timesharing computer" is used to refer to a mini or mainframe computer which has a large capacity operating system and is designed to service multiple users simultaneously.

"LAN" or ***"Local Area Network"*** refers to a system for networking microcomputers so that they can share printing and storage devices including stored software and data. A LAN may also permit microcomputers to share a gateway to WANs (Wide Area Networks).

"PBX" or ***"Public Branch Exchange"*** is a switch which acts as a communications network hub with individual channels to each user station. A PBX is designed to serve a local area, such as a building complex or campus. A modern digital PBX can switch digitized data, digitized voice and compressed digitized video between stations.

Of course, where necessary and appropriate, trade names are used to refer to the equipment installed at Northwest. Such mention does not constitute an endorsement. We are grateful to Dr. Phillip Heeler and Robert Henry for reading a draft of our manuscript and for supplying valuable information and insights throughout, and we appreciate the efforts of Lisa Swartz for her assistance in producing many of the graphs and pie charts. Carole Gieseke displayed her normal adeptness in designing and laying out the book. We also express our gratitude to the members of the Computing Services and Telecommunications staff for their faithful team effort and unwavering commitment to collect and analyze data about The Northwest Electronic Campus. Finally, we dedicate this book to the students, faculty and staff of Northwest Missouri State University who have committed time, energy and unusual amounts of inventiveness to making the Northwest Electronic Campus a dynamic and ever-growing tool for education at all levels and in all disciplines.

Jon T. Rickman
Dean L. Hubbard

Maryville, Missouri
April 24, 1992

BUILDING THE FOUNDATIONS

One

1

THE SETTING

The old adage that "form follows function" applies to the design of computer systems as surely as it does to the design of buildings or organizational structures. Much of the national attention Northwest Missouri State University has received because of its Electronic Campus has been predicated on the assumption that what has been done is a model that could (or should) be implemented elsewhere. While every institution has unique features which must be considered when any change or innovation is contemplated, the "functions" of a majority of post-secondary institutions in America overlap when it comes to the way computers may be used on campus. This fact notwithstanding, variables such as size, student body composition, programmatic focus, and the percentage of students housed on campus need to be carefully compared and contrasted before one institution's approach is adopted by another. The purpose of this chapter is to describe Northwest Missouri State University along these dimensions so that other educators can decide how close the fit really is to their own environment.

PROFILE OF NORTHWEST MISSOURI STATE UNIVERSITY.

As a comprehensive, co-educational, publicly supported regional university, Northwest shares a history common to most state universities in the nation. Founded in 1905 as a normal school, the institution expanded its offerings following World War II and was granted university status by the Missouri General Assembly in 1972. The four colleges around which the University is organizationally structured reflect the institution's primary focus: College of Agriculture, Science and Technology; College of Arts and Humanities; College of Business, Government and Computer Science; and College of Education. The 24 departments which make up the four colleges house four certificate programs, 28 bachelor of arts, 78 bachelor of science, and 32 master's degree programs plus the educational specialist degree. Business is the largest program, followed by education, mass communications/speech, psychology/ sociology, agriculture and computer science.

The University is governed by a seven-member, state-appointed Board of Regents. For 1991-92, state support amounted to $3,264 per full-time equivalent student. In-state students paid $2,118 per semester which included tuition, textbook rental for University-owned textbooks, food, housing, computer, telephone and television services. Standard computer services include a terminal with a timesharing account, a telephone line with voice mail services and a video hookup in each residence hall room.

Northwest had a Fall 1991 student enrollment of 6,021 (5,273 FTE). The majority of full-time undergraduate students (53 percent) live on campus in 13 residence halls and come from within a 100-mile radius of Maryville, Missouri (population: 10,658), where the University is located. All classroom buildings and residence halls are located on a campus of 288 contiguous acres (see campus map, Appendix A) which was originally developed as a nursery in 1857 by horticulturist Capt. Thomas W. Gaunt. More than 75 varieties of trees and abundant, beautiful bluegrass contribute to a pastoral atmosphere on the campus which is neither traversed with roads nor hemmed in on all sides by housing.

Seventy-nine percent of first-time freshmen live in the 1,493 residence hall rooms. (University policy requires most freshmen to live on campus.) A common complaint is that the rooms, which typically house two students, are too crowded and lack surplus desktop space. This is nothing new for many similar institutions with housing structures built in the 1960s.

Northwest has consciously and deliberately structured a large proportion of its environment and programs to serve full-time students who wish to study in a residential campus environment. The University also delivers networking services to off-campus and non-traditional students through multiple laboratories in the library and several classroom buildings. To extend computer access to faculty at home, students, and the northwest Missouri region, more than 20 traditional dial-up modems are maintained. The University also has made a conscious effort to limit its enrollment to its current size, around 6,000 students.

COMPUTING AND THE MISSION OF NORTHWEST.

The University's statement of mission commits it to "provide a quality living-learning environment which will equip the individual for responsible participation in a rapidly changing society." The statement goes on to assert that "throughout the University, students are taught to gather, organize, analyze and synthesize information, to think coherently, and to speak and write clearly." These commitments have led Northwest to declare that its graduates should "be as comfortable with the computer as their parents are with the telephone." This requires convenient access and a particular kind of focus for computing on campus: namely, a focus on the way professionals use computers in non-computer-related disciplines.

Each entering student receives his or her own Electronic Campus Service Card which includes a computer username and telephone authorization code.

At Northwest, computers are not the object of study; computing is not the object of study; nor is computer assisted instruction (CAI) the primary object of study. Rather, the computer is seen as a utility for all students, faculty and staff. In this context, computing is approached from five perspectives. First, the Electronic Campus system was designed to be a tool primarily for students. Northwest freshmen receive an Electronic Campus Service Card (pictured) and are eligible for electronic services as soon as they matriculate. They retain their computer accounts until they graduate. Students are trained and encouraged to frequently use the various tools available on the system.

Second, the computer is seen as an aid in learning. Various applications reflecting this perspective have been purchased or developed for the system. Third, the computer is developed as a tool for the faculty. They too are heavy users of the common features of the system plus applications designed especially for them. Fourth, the computer is used as an aid in teaching. Finally, the computer is seen as an aid in administering the University. On-line self registration and standard accounting and reporting data functions illustrate this focus.

AN OVERVIEW OF THE NORTHWEST ELECTRONIC CAMPUS.

Although details regarding Northwest's Electronic Campus are presented in later chapters, the following overview highlights ways in which the system was matched to the University's environment.

The Northwest Electronic Campus is a functionally integrated system of computer, telephone and television networks designed for the academic user in a university environment. As seen in Figure 1, the network delivers comprehensive data, voice and video services including word processing, electronic publishing, electronic spreadsheet with graphics processing, world-wide electronic mail and voice communications. On-line retrieval systems provide access to the library bibliographic catalog, an encyclopedia, abstracts of periodicals, campus news, University calendars and directories; enrollment, transcript, student and financial data; job and scholarship information; and a career advisement database and bulletin boards. In addition, there are picture, synthesized voice, digitized voice and full motion video retrieval systems. Optional electronic services for residence hall students include letter-quality printers and additional television channels. Dial-up on-line library catalog searches and inter-library loan services are also provided to area colleges and area high schools.

Fifteen traditional academic microcomputer laboratories complement the Northwest Electronic Campus and are distributed throughout classroom buildings and the library to support specialized academic software, CAI courseware and applications which have rigid hardware or operating system platform requirements. Traditional radio and television satellite receivers, compressed video conferencing rooms, broadcasting systems, camera studios and editing laboratories augment the automated Electronic Campus television channels.

The University's Department of Computing Services and Telecommunications is responsible for all computing and telecommunications hardware plus all timesharing, networking, and telecommunications software management. Academic departments are responsible for microcomputer software and operating the laboratories associated with their department. Administrative departments are responsible for collecting, updating, and insuring the privacy of the data needed by their department with software development and maintenance provided by Computing Services and Telecommunications.

Northwest Electronic Campus Menu of Services

INFO	**Information Retrieval System** campus calendar, scholarships, student and staff directories, class openings, jobs, usernames, tutors
TEXT	**Text Retrieval System** news, encyclopedia, readers guide, computing guide, library catalog
PICT	**Picture Retrieval System** campus and building maps, electronic networks, art
VIDEO	**Video Retrieval System** computing services, library services, science, calendar marquee
VOICE	**Voice Retrieval System** class openings, budgets, calendar
DESK	**Personal Desktop Tools** calendar, addresses, calculator
BULL	**Bulletin Boards** VAX services, PC software, user-requested topics
MAIL	**Electronic Mail System** NOWnet, MOREnet, Internet, BITNET
MESS	**Voice Message System** store, play, edit, append, send
WORD	**Word Processing System** spelling dictionary, thesaurus, personal publisher, file cabinet
SHEET	**Electronic Spreadsheet** line, bar, and pie graphs
FILE	**File Processing Tools** edit, display, print, delete, copy, directory, WATCOM basic
CAI	**Computer Aided Instruction** history, chemistry, government
SCI	**Scientific Computing Services** SAS statistical analysis and graph, MODULA 2, PROLOG, LISP, OPS5, FORTRAN, C, PASCAL, COBOL, RDB, ADA, Authoring
SIGI	**Student Career Guidance System** careers, colleges, degrees
SYS	**System Management Tools** change password, help, show free disk, connects, maintenance days, long distance telephone rates
LAN	**Local Area Network Services** MICROVAX Server for MS-DOS and MAC, RISC workstations
STAR	**Student Transcript and Records** student self enroll, class schedule, transcript, degree audit, phone and print bill, cashiering bill
WORK	**Staff Support Systems** student transcripts and schedule, teacher class rolls, gradebook with test scoring and analysis, budgets
ADMIN	**Administrative Systems** admissions, textbooks, grades, financial aid, loans, placement, alumni, ordering, payables, payrolls, ledger, receivables, facility and meeting scheduling, ticket sales
BYE	**Logoff and Disconnect**

Figure 1

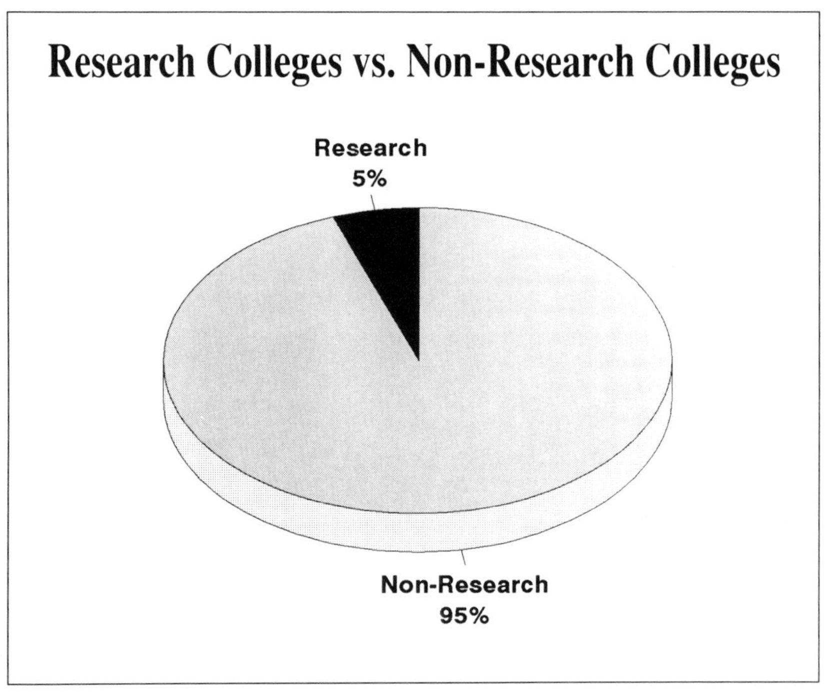

Figure 2

SUMMARY AND CONCLUSIONS.

When the topic of providing adequate computer resources for students is discussed, the research university is often cited as representative of the challenges faced by educational decision makers.[1,2] In fact, this type of institution is not typical of most institutions, either in terms of resources available or the needs of the majority of students. Such institutions frequently have enrollments ranging from 20,000 to 35,000 students, large numbers of graduate students, a strong commitment to basic research, and operate on multiple campuses.

Understandably, their computing strategy has typically centered on microcomputers tied together through Local Area Networks (LANs).

---

[1] Arms, Caroline. *Campus Networking Strategies*, 1988

[2] McCredie, John W. *Campus Computing Strategies*

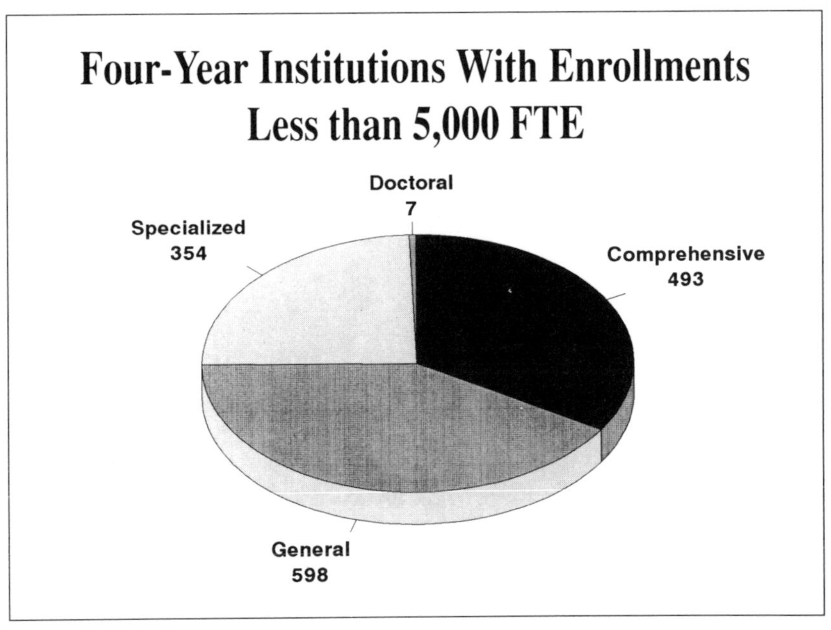

Figure 3

However, as shown in Figure 2, in the United States 94.9 percent of higher educational institutions are non-research; only 5.1 percent are classified as research. Likewise, only 21.7 percent enroll more than 5,000 full-time-equivalent students;[3] 78.3 percent have under 5,000 students. Clearly, from Figure 3, there is a need for a computing resources model which will meet the needs of this large group of non-research, smaller institutions. We believe Northwest's Electronic Campus represents such a model for many general and comprehensive four-year institutions.

---

[3] AASCU 1986 Report. Source: U.S. Department of Education, Center for Education Statistics. "Fall Enrollment in Colleges and Universities, 1985" survey.

2

BUILDING AN INFRASTRUCTURE

Even as institutions are in some sense held captive by their past, the decision to install a comprehensive innovation such as an Electronic Campus must take into account the legacy left by previous choices in the area of computing. For example, if an institution has a long history of distributed funding and management of computing, then political as well as hardware issues will have to be resolved before moving ahead. It is for this reason that we have included a brief history of computing at Northwest, noting critical choices and events that created a readiness for installation of the system which was ultimately deployed. In this chapter we trace events and decisions leading up to the actual installation of the Electronic Campus. The next chapter picks the story up at the point when the actual decision to install was made. In both chapters we detail some of the more obstinate administrative problems encountered along the way (technical problems are discussed in chapters six and seven). The hope is that by tracing the experiences of Northwest, other institutions may be able to anticipate some of the challenges they will encounter if they decide to pursue a similar strategy.

A RESOURCE SHARING AND TIMESHARING TRADITION.

Northwest Missouri State University may not have moved as completely and quickly as it did from batch computing to timesharing and interactive computing had it not been for a tragic fire. Although as early as 1978 – under new computing leadership – the Computing Services Department began repositioning itself in terms of basic computing resources by installing a timesharing minicomputer and several dozen 8-bit microcomputers, a devastating fire on July 24, 1979, definitely hastened the process.

The fire started on the fourth floor of the Administration Building and rapidly spread to within a few feet of the first floor computer center. While the blaze was still on the upper floors, and moments before tons of water poured down from the hoses above, fire fighters were able to secure tarpaulins over the University's Digital Equipment Corporation (DEC) PDP 11/70 timesharing computer. As reported in *ComputerWorld*, within 24 hours the PDP was removed from several inches of water, relocated in the science building, and reconnected. After the fire, the University's IBM 360 batch processing mainframe was never restarted, leaving the campus truly committed to interactive computing, even though for several more years a cardless remote job entry system on the PDP did permit limited access to mainframe computers at the University of Missouri in Columbia.

Northwest's commitment to high access, interactive personalized computing was also initiated in 1978 when it became one of the first universities in Missouri to locate a computer laboratory in every class-room building on campus. Built around three VAX 700 series timesharing computers, in the early 1980s services were also extended to the local

Maryville high school via a MICOM model 600 data PBX and several long distance line drivers. High speed computer-to-computer Local Area Networking over DECnet came into daily use in early 1980s.

Timesharing computers were first introduced on campus to serve scientific and word processing needs, a perspective reflected in the software available to early users of the system. In fact, in those early days even administrative applications, which frequently enjoy first priority, were not addressed (even when timesharing COBOL became available) because of a shortage of competent database management systems.

Later, after an aborted attempt to program an administrative system in BASIC, a table-driven and menu-operated file manager system using indexed sequential files was written in COBOL. This package, named DATAMAIN, which took two months for a systems programmer and a programmer analyst to program in 1981, has been in constant, heavy use ever since. With "create," "update," "display," "search," "select," "sort," "report," "print address labels" and "transfer addresses to word processing" functions available, DATAMAIN has permitted a small programming staff to stay ahead of administrative demands for application development. This, in turn, has permitted the programming staff to concentrate on the development of some very interesting public access information retrieval systems which students and faculty have found helpful in an academic environment.

Two early and fortuitous decisions were critical to creating an environment congenial to the Electronic Campus: (1) the establishment of minimum performance standards; and (2), a mandate that equipment must be compatible. Although committees are not noted for their capacity to make restrictive decisions, the Northwest Academic Computing Committee of 1983 was an outstanding counter-example. They voted to accept the DEC VT100 terminal, or its emulation by a microcomputer, as the minimum benchmark against which any proposed user-station must be measured. This decision ensured that every computing station on campus would be capable of communicating with the computing center. It also saved untold time and dollars in all future networking efforts.

DEVELOPING "UTILITY" SOFTWARE.

Firmly repositioned with user friendly interactive computing systems, the University concentrated on developing a set of data retrieval systems which would provide public access to current information in local databanks for all students, faculty and administrators. An objective was that whenever possible and practical, the system would be designed so that users wishing to access information would not be restricted to standard keyboards, but would also be able to use touch screens, graphics screens and touch tone telephones for inputting requests.

During the first half of the 1980s, cable TV was installed in the remaining uncabled residence halls. This move set the stage for computer and telephone wiring which would complete the infrastructure necessary to support a comprehensive Electronic Campus.

In 1984, Amoco Oil Company supported the development of a touch-tone telephone public information system using DECtalk, Digital Equipment Corporation's text-to-voice synthesizer. This system accesses live databases stored anywhere in the computer network and reports instantly via the DECtalk voice synthesizer. For example, using touch-tone telephones off campus or in their rooms, students can key in the catalog course number and be told the number of seats available in that class. Also, administrators can be apprised of an up-to-the-minute balance in budget accounts. Altogether, nine types of information can be gleaned through the touch-tone telephone talker. In similar fashion, digitized voice messages can be retrieved from one or more of the 4,000 voice mailboxes on the system.

At the same time a computer-generated voice system was being developed, the University was expanding video offerings into residence hall rooms through two cable channels. As part of the Electronic Campus, one of these channels is used to broadcast video instructional materials which are stored on laser discs and retrieved through terminals on the VAX system network.

The steady development of the electronic utilities at Northwest is shown as a timeline of activity (see Appendix B). This timeline shows a committment to building campus data networks which approach 100 percent connectivity of **buildings** in the early 1980s to building campus data networks which approach 100 percent **room** connectivity in the mid 1980s. In the late 1980s the telephone network embraced the 100 percent connectivity model and in the early 1990s the committment is shown for world-wide connectivity of data, voice and video.

SUMMARY AND CONCLUSIONS.

It has long been accepted in the telephone industry that the value of a network is proportional to the number of people or applications one can access. A telephone system which only connects 50 percent of a population has less value than one which connects 100 percent of a population. Likewise, the decision to provide "100 percent connectivity" on the Northwest campus dramatically increased the usage and value of the system to the campus community. This decision built upon, and in many respects was a natural extension of, a series of decisions that had been made over a 10-year period. Campus-wide political support for equal access to electronic services by everyone is easy to secure if individuals and departments can identify common needs, or services the authors consider to be utilities. While it would certainly not be impossible for an institution to make a radical change from past practices, if this is necessary, the political as well as technical environment must be carefully studied and managed.

3

INSTALLING THE ELECTRONIC CAMPUS

Soon after the inauguration of Dean Hubbard as president in the fall of 1984, Northwest Missouri State University developed a plan to equip every faculty office and student residence hall room with a computer terminal and full telephone services. Both of these components were served and interfaced through the University's clustered timesharing VAX computers. When the system became fully operational in 1987, the result was an Electronic Campus made up of 2,300 terminals plus over 500 microcomputers in departmental laboratories and faculty offices.

The Electronic Campus features an integrated system of computer, telephone and television networks designed for the academic user. Pictured is an early application of the Electronic Campus, Fall 1986.

THE GOALS OF THE SYSTEM.

Early in the planning stages two critical commitments were made which have guided the development of the Electronic Campus ever since. First, the needs of students take precedence over administrative needs; and second, the system is structured around a centralized cluster of timesharing computers. Within the context of those commitments the University adopted three goals related to computer proficiency: (1) To ensure that students gain a working knowledge of the computer, particularly skill in accessing databases; (2) To improve student writing skills through convenient access to word processing, editors, dictionaries, a thesaurus and an encyclopedia; and (3) To improve communications on campus through the use of electronic mail between and among residence hall rooms, faculty offices and administrative services. Pursuing these goals led to providing access to the library card catalog from residence hall rooms and faculty offices; providing instructional video materials which can be scheduled on the computer; providing easy access to text editing, spreadsheets and other common software packages; and making available various marquees and databases such as daily/weekly calendars, announcements, scholarship directory, student job openings and student/staff directories.

Faculty surveys showed strong support for such comprehensive computing services. Subsequently, a major faculty training effort was launched in 1986. The Computer Science department taught 30 sections of basic computing and word processing for faculty. These sessions, organized around individual academic departmental needs, had more than 80 percent attendance in the first series, and through make-up sessions provided training for all faculty. Faculty offices were wired and had operational terminals by the spring of 1987, one semester before terminals were installed in the residence halls. This lead time was important for several reasons. First of all, it helped to alleviate anxieties that students would jump ahead of and embarrass faculty. Second, it prepared the faculty to help students transition to the new environment. Third, it gave faculty time to prepare assignments which utilized the system, and thus conferred immediate credibility and relevance on the system. Finally, it converted most (though not all) of the few remaining naysayers among the faculty who questioned the wisdom of making such a large investment of time and money.

INSTALLING THE SYSTEM.

To say the least, the procurement and installation of a data network with 100 percent connectivity for each campus colleague constituted a major challenge. Not surprisingly, an indispensable threshold issue was money, both capital to cover the initial cost of wiring and hardware, and operating funds to keep the system up-to-date and functioning smoothly. A related constraint was the need to design a system which would function effectively in a state institution funded at about $7,500 per student per year (including student tuition), versus more than $20,000 for many private institutions or doctoral-granting research institutions which have made strides in campus networking. Within these constraints, an initial capital budget of $2.5 million was set as the target for the project.

Against this backdrop, the University launched the project by seeking bids to trench and install cable across the entire campus. The procurement specifications also included the purchase of a digital telephone PBX (Public Branch Exchange which serves as a local-area voice and/or data switch). After a full year of writing specifications and listening to vendors avoid pricing commitments, three bids were received. The disappointment on campus was palpable when the lowest qualifying bid came in at about $3 million for just a telephone system, more than what had been estimated for the entire project. Needless to say, all bids were refused while those responsible for designing the project returned to the drawing boards.

A new plan was developed which actually saw the computing goals expanded while some of the telephone goals were delayed. Under this new plan, the University became the general contractor which awarded bids for underground conduiting, tunnel trays, and new cable for voice and data networks. A separate contract for interior wiring of the residence halls was also developed. This contract was awarded to the United Telephone of Missouri at $142 per room to install dual J11 modular jacks and four pairs of copper conductors in conduit from each room to the basement of each residence hall. All classroom and office buildings were similarly wired by two employees of the University's telecommunications staff.

Some 20 T1 (1.54 million bits per second) trunking circuits were installed to connect buildings to the expanded data PBXs. Each of these T1 circuits could carry 128 multiplexed individual data paths to the data PBXs in the computer center. The computer center had been relocated to the basement of the University's new library, which provided new power and air conditioning systems plus easy access to the utility tunnel.

One interesting and creative cost cutting measure was to entice the varsity football team to pull the huge, heavy, 1200 pair copper voice cables through the quarter-mile-long service tunnel which traverses the campus. The football team worked hard for two hours and did an exemplary job, but they were surprised how much muscle was required. (Actually, we claim the workout may have contributed to their excellent record that year!)

Further cost-cutting measures involved purchasing refurbished or nearly new computers whenever possible. Also, Digital Equipment Corporation provided substantial discounts for many components of the VAX cluster of timesharing computers and a grant of 300 graphics

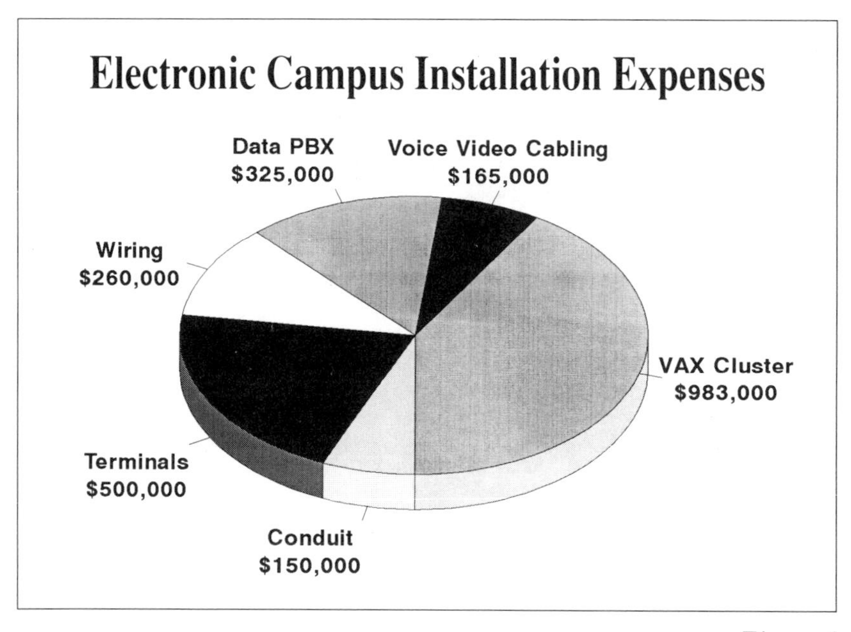

Figure 4

terminals for faculty offices.

Since a voice PBX could not be purchased during the first round of bidding, and since voice Centrex services were not yet offered by the telephone central office in Maryville, the system went on line in 1987 with only optional telephone services available. Students were encouraged to contract with the local telephone company for service to their room using University cabling and wiring. Also, by that year, DECnet LAN services were supported by a high-speed fiber optics Ethernet network connecting all VAX timesharing computers and VAX workstations.

By the time the system was ready for initial high access use, $2.4 million had been spent. Of that amount, $1,183,000 had been appropriated by the Missouri legislature. The balance came from a loan which required a $25 per semester increase in residence hall fees to pay back. Additional funds were received from private resources and equipment vendors. The breakout of project expenditures is shown in the pie chart (Figure 4).

Missouri Gov. John Ashcroft (at center in the top photo) was joined by other state dignitaries in "switching on" the Electronc Campus before a crowd of 2000 in August 1987. In the photo at right, Gov. Ashcroft participated in a demonstration of the system given by student Stacy Lee and President Hubbard. During the demonstration, the governor quipped, "This computer system spells things out in such detail that even the governor ...can run it!"

A big celebration was planned for August 17, 1987, to inaugurate the Electronic Campus. A large symbolic switch was constructed on a platform in front of the Administration Building so the governor of Missouri could ceremonially "switch on" the system. An assembly was planned for the new freshman class along with their parents, legislators, community and campus leaders. However, Murphy's Law seemed to be working in the old Administration Building once again: Three days before the big day, August 14, a mega-volt lightning storm hit Maryville and fried 16 terminals in the Administration Building. Fortunately, everything was repaired, Gov. John Aschroft arrived, switched the system on in the presence of 2,000 guests, and was welcomed to campus by the voice synthesizer. Later in the morning, he sat down to a computing station in a residence hall and successfully used the system.

RECENT ENHANCEMENTS TO THE SYSTEM.

Since initial installation, the exterior point-to-point fiber optic Ethernet LAN has been upgraded to include a fiber optic hub to expand the campus network backbone. The interior Ethernet LAN cabling has been upgraded from thick coax to thin coax to provide servers and connectivity for 32-bit microcomputers. Ethernet is reserved for connecting the more powerful computers. Slower 16-bit microcomputers and terminals are restricted to connections via the dual data PBXs. The PBXs provide 3,000 asynchronous channels for user station communications. The only use of traditional dial-in modems is for off-campus users.

In 1989, a Centrex telephone system – based on the Maryville Central Office Northern Telecom DMS-100 switch – replaced the University-owned Harris PBX which could only support faculty and staff telephone use. The new service was installed in every office and residence hall room, thus fulfilling the original goal of providing 100 percent voice connectivity. A telephone system billing port for optional long distance service was also added to the network. Computers were programmed to look up long distance charges for calls made and display them on the student's computer terminal. In fact, another option in the same system permits anyone to retrieve and display the charge for making a call before

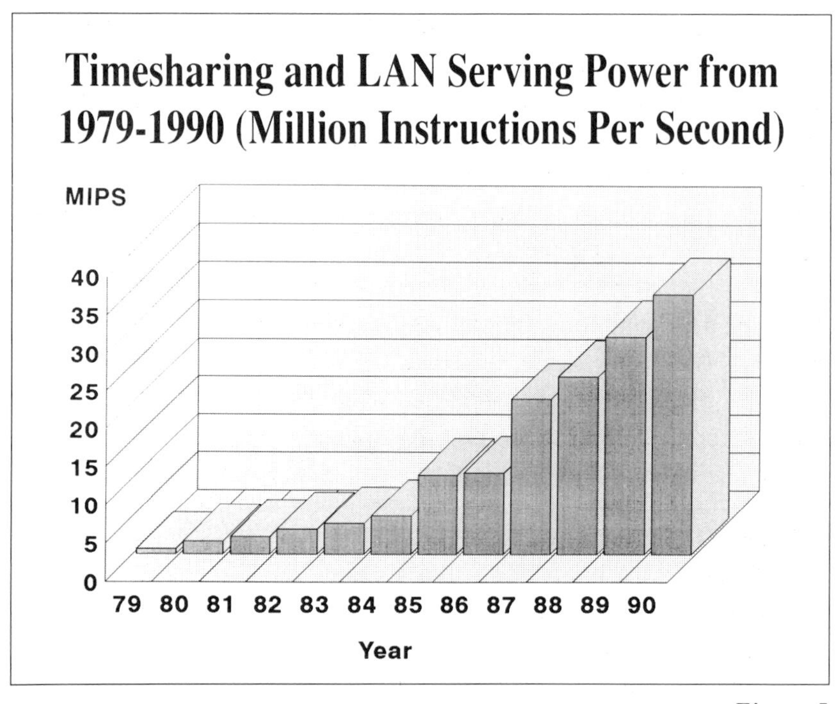

Figure 5

dialing or to check the geographic location (city or town) of a specific telephone area code and exchange code.

Throughout the 1980s, many specialized interactive or graphics applications were off-loaded to run in one of 15 University and departmental microcomputer laboratories. These laboratories contain seven microVAXs, about 40 Apple MACs, and about 125 MS-DOS compatible microcomputers, 70 with the 386 processor and VGA graphics.

In 1989 user demand for library applications outgrew the capacity of the old PDP 11/70 library computer running the LS/2000 software package. The system was upgraded to a VAX-based system which permitted the sharing of its database through clustering, thus giving six computers and their users access to the library search systems. A used VAX computer and ATLAS library automation software costing nearly $170,000 were installed to complete the upgrade.

By 1991, mass storage systems for databases and accounts had grown steadily to a capacity of 17 billion characters. The network had also grown to support another 200 interactive terminals in additional residence hall rooms and laboratories made necessary by enrollment growth. As shown in Figure 5, for 12 years, 1979 thru 1990, Northwest's 32-bit timesharing and LAN server power was expanded from 1 MIPS (million instructions per second) to 41 MIPS, with only a little more than 2 MIPS of this resource being retired.

Not suprisingly, timesharing and microcomputers with less than 32-bit word lengths have slowly become obsolete in terms of their ability to support modern software. The direct cause for obsolescence has been the expanding size of modern software applications and their corresponding need for large address spaces. Consistent with this trend, microcomputer operating systems which support only 16-bit addresses will also face obsolescence in the near future. In the 1990s, as we see the microcomputer implementation of 64-bit technology, we will again see the familiar eclipse of current 32-bit hardware and software systems.

PROBLEMS.

Needless to say, problems were encountered throughout the project. Fortunately, none were fatal. Four, however, deserve mention. The first is funding. Some wise observer suggested that University presidents are people who live in big houses and beg for money! Between 1985 and 1987 the president of Northwest and the development staff made scores of contacts on behalf of the Electronic Campus. Every key legislator who would vote on the funding request was visited at least once in his or her office. Additionally, the governor and key members of his staff, along with the commissioner of higher education and members of the Coordinating Board for Higher Education, were lobbied. Alumni meetings were held across the country and foundations were solicited. Fortunately, since nearly everyone was intrigued by the possibility of an Electronic Campus at Northwest, necessary funds were secured.

Since the system has gone on line, a second type of problem has

Computing Station Distribution

General Purpose Timesharing Access	
On-campus Student Residence Hall Rooms	1500 Terminals 40 Printers
Laboratories for Off-campus Students (7)	110 Terminals 5 Line Printers 8 Laser Printers
Faculty Offices and Labs	270 Terminals 75 PCs 320 Printers
Staff Offices and Library	490 Terminals 165 PCs 270 Printers
Personal Computer Laboratories on LANS	
Library Academic Computing	4 PCs
Business Laboratory	22 PCs
Science Laboratories (4)	40 PCs
Industrial Technology	14 PCs
Graphic Design	8 MACs
Mass Communication	25 MACs
Personal Computer Laboratories Stand-alones	
Library Academic Computing	8 PCs
Tutoring Center	3 PCs 3 MACs
Science Laboratory	10 MACs
Business Laboratories	30 PCs
Agriculture	10 PCs
Music	4 PCs
Psychology	4 PCs
Human Environmental Sciences	4 Apples
Elementary Laboratory School	24 Apples

Figure 6

emerged from time to time that must be addressed; namely, the tendency to compromise the original focus for the system. Specifically, it is easy to forget the commitment that student access and convenience must come first. While faculty with legitimate and demonstrated research needs are provided powerful computing stations in their offices or laboratories, occasionally some individual or group will mount pressure to divert resources to satisfy what appears to be nothing more than an idiosyncratic desire for the latest equipment reaching the marketplace. Occasionally, microcomputers intended for laboratories end up in faculty offices. The policy has been to avoid purchasing highly specialized and expensive equipment that clearly provides a capacity that exceeds the users' needs or will have very narrow and only occasional application. Obviously, some of these systems can be justified and there is no single answer to this problem; constant diligence is required.

A similar, but less troublesome, challenge results from the fact that as faculty become more proficient with the computer they discover more esoteric applications which they naturally want to introduce to their students. Since many of these applications are only applicable to one course, and maybe only a limited number of class sessions within that course, it is not practical to reprogram them to run on any platform other than the one for which they were originally programmed.

In order to respond to these special needs, the University established 15 labs, distributed as shown in Figure 6, situated near faculty who use them in their instruction. However, it was soon discovered that even this approach does not completely ameliorate the access problem. When lower-division students are required to use these labs, access problems develop not unlike those found on most campuses: long student lines waiting for remote laboratories to be opened or for microcomputers to become available. Students have complained about this problem and faculty are trying to limit, as far as possible, specialized applications to upper division students. Also, it was discovered that some so-called special software applications were nothing more than a different vendor's version of an application already available on the timesharing computers.

Finally, a slowly but steadily growing problem is related to purchasing equipment from the lowest bidder. This problem is not new to public institutions. However, contrary to popular biases, both items of equipment causing problems – dot-matrix printers and terminal keyboards – were not manufactured in the United States of America. Over 600 return keys, costing $1.75 each, have broken on the keyboards from one manufacturer and far too many print heads have failed on one vendors' printers! After five years of use, some of these pieces of equipment need to be replaced by higher quality units.

All of these problems were anticipated. However, no one expected what would happen once everyone on campus had access to electronic mail (E-mail). In 1985, when Northwest first experimented with computing services in residence halls, there was little interest in E-mail. But when the critical mass, or threshold, of users was reached with over 2,000 stations on the network, an E-mail frenzy developed. Within days, demand surged to exceed system capacity every evening about 10:00 p.m. and for several hours later. E-mail became for many students – particularly freshmen – the preferred avenue for initiating social contacts, especially with the opposite sex. Demand for this feature continues to be high even though it was moderated by about 10,000 messages per week with the implementation of voice mail boxes for every student, staff and faculty member on campus. What happened probably portends what society at large could experience when E-mail is as common as the telephone or mail box (if no usage charge is implemented).

Another initial problem, which seems to continue for the less goal-oriented students, was also associated with E-mail. There developed a small group of students (a dozen or less) in the residence halls who seemed obsessed with E-mail, spending eight to twelve hours a day on the system. "E-mail mania," as it came to be called, affected several of these students so profoundly that they neglected academic responsibilities to the point of failure. Although this obsession is probably no different than addiction to video or microcomputer games, it is a situation that has to be reckoned with.

Several steps were taken to control E-mail. First, a time limit of 20 minutes was set for E-mail use. When it expires, the student has to log-in again. Second, an on-line directory was developed so users could know the identity of any sender. This greatly reduced unwelcomed obscenities and harassment. Third, the number of ports supporting E-mail was limited to 90.

Analyzing the quantitative use of E-mail has been relatively easy in the timesharing environment as compared to a network of microcomputers. It is also relatively easy to restrict E-mail access to six or seven times a day or charge for its use if it is determined to be desirable or appropriate.

Further discussion of E-mail can be found in Chapter 5, "The Impact on Students."

SUMMARY AND CONCLUSIONS.

Several obvious lessons can be learned from Northwest's experience. First, even though the number of failure points (e.g., miles of wire, thousands of switches, et cetera) is astronomical, such a system can be installed and maintained within the resources available to a moderately-sized university. Northwest's overall system worked nearly flawlessly from day one and has continued to serve the campus with almost no unscheduled down-time. Obviously, this track record reflects a focused and redundant system design and an alert and competent computer staff. Second, the system is flexible and modular enough so that it has been able to grow and expand to meet technological changes and advances as well as growing needs and levels of sophistication on the part of students and faculty. Third, the system now enjoys universal enthusiasm among faculty and students and has proved to be an obvious asset in recruiting new faculty and students.

4

ELECTRONIC CAMPUS SERVICES AVAILABLE

In keeping with its focus on computing as a utility, Northwest is constantly adding general interest applications to the Electronic Campus. Indeed, Northwest students, faculty and staff have access to one of the largest collections of user-friendly, accessible databases available on any campus in the nation. A variety of devices can be used to access this information. While most electronic services are available through the ubiquitous keyboards found on campus, many may be accessed using a combination of devices. For example, campus maps, building profiles and floor plans can be accessed on either of two computer-driven Touch Screen Color Graphics Directories located near the main entrance of the library and on the main floor of the Administration

A Touch Screen Color Graphics Directory is located on the main floor of the Administration Building, allowing access to campus maps, building profiles, and floor plans. A second directory is located near the front entrance of Owens Library.

Building (pictured) or on any of over 1,000 graphics terminals on campus. Other databases may be reached from on- or off-campus touch tone telephones or through keyboards. Video applications are available on dedicated television channels and are scheduled via any keyboard in the network.

This chapter describes some typical services available through timesharing computers at Northwest as well as some of the more significant University-supplied applications available in specialized microcomputer labs.

NORTHWEST'S SOFTWARE DEVELOPMENT STRATEGY.

While hardware system growth came in a burst following legislative funding of the Electronic Campus, Northwest's strategy has been to steadily and incrementally build software systems specially tailored to a residential campus. This effort has continued for more than 10 years and is proceeding unabated today.

The overriding concern for any publicly accessed system should be to design a "friendly" system; that is, one as easy as possible for the beginner to use. One of the better ways to achieve this goal is to make extensive use of menus (optional where possible for experienced users). When a user turns on the computer, he or she should not face a blank screen. The importance of this single feature was dramatically illustrated when graduating seniors were interviewed. They were asked to choose between WPS (Digital Equipment Corporation's Word Processing System) and WordPerfect 5.1 word processing systems. They opted for WPS over the more elegant WordPerfect for the single reason that the latter in its default configuration presents the user with a blank screen while WPS brings up a menu.

Obviously, users can work their way through a system of menus easier than they can through blank screens. (Students also said that their real concern was learning "word processing," not some particular vendor's application, an astute observation still not made by some administrators, faculty or employers.) The Electronic Campus network is traversed by user-friendly menus from which users select the application they want to run and by applications themselves which also are menu driven.

This strategy has had a major impact on network design and on the choice of equipment for the system. After extensive evaluation of available terminal servers by Northwest staff, several were determined to be "unfriendly;" that is, too esoteric for the beginner. Some terminal servers were also unable to queue requests for network connects when resources were at maximum load (in the same way a modern telephone system can automatically call again later if a line is busy), and these servers required frustrating repeated manual attempts to make network connections.

ENTERING THE SYSTEM.

After matriculation to Northwest, each student must sign a Computing Service Agreement – a contract for Electronic Campus service – and a Telecommunications Agreement. The latest version of this contract is

Examples of Northwest Electronic Campus Computer Screens

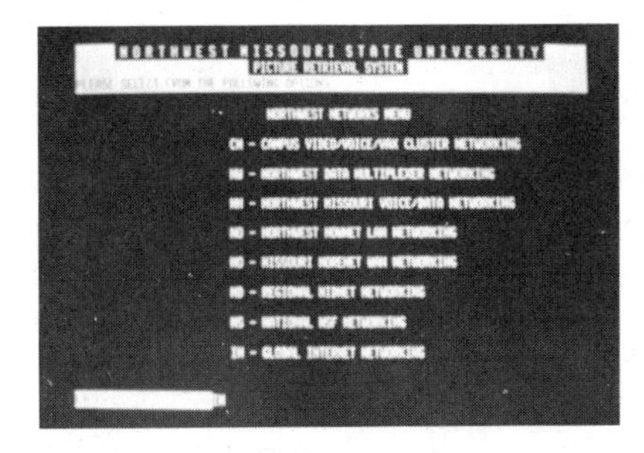

Picture Retrieval System Menu

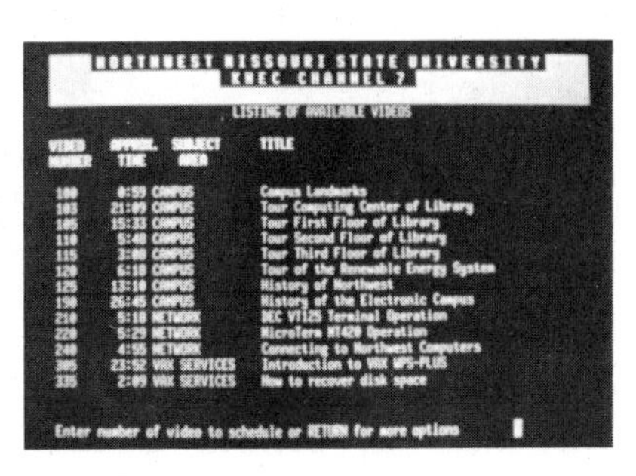

Videodisc Menu

Retrieved Picture

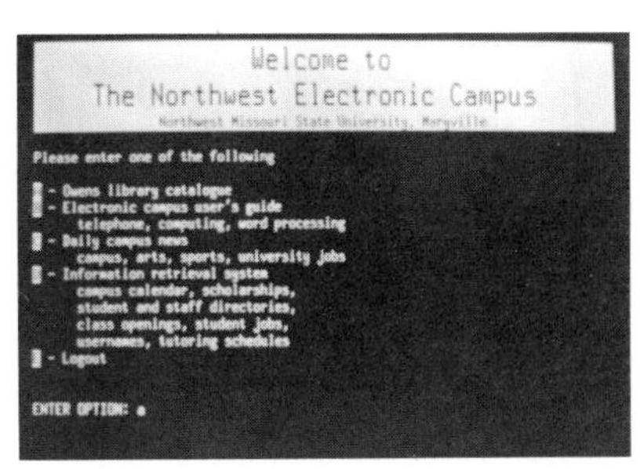

Guest Menu

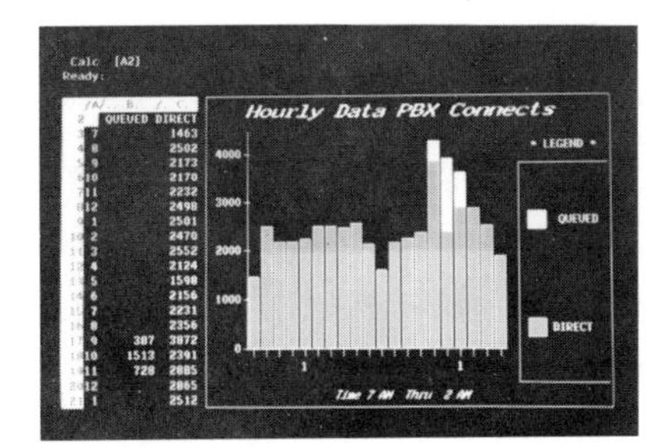

Spreadsheet Graph

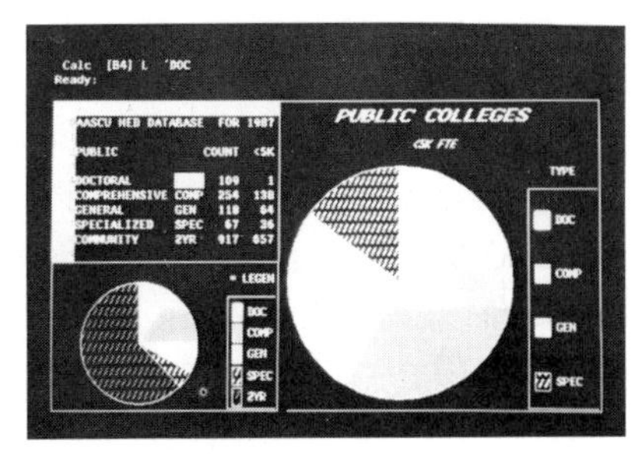

Spreadsheet Pie Chart

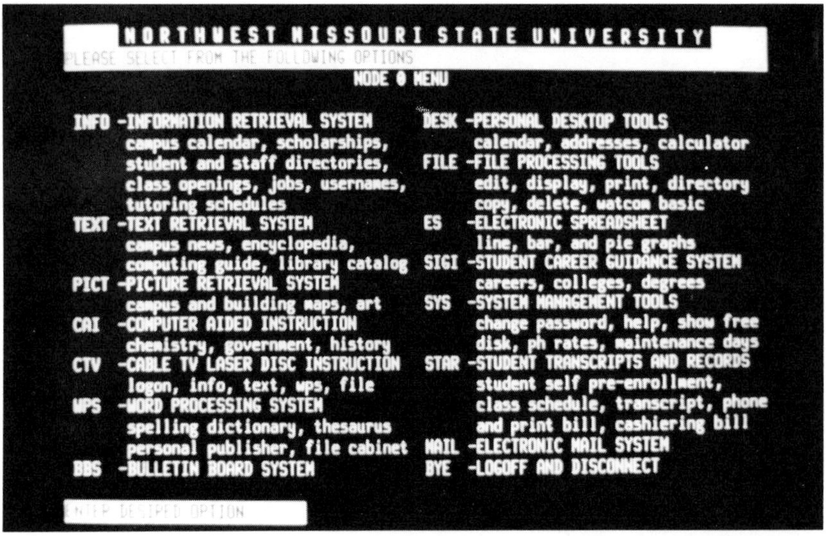

NORTHWEST MISSOURI STATE UNIVERSITY
PLEASE SELECT FROM THE FOLLOWING OPTIONS
MODE 0 MENU

INFO -INFORMATION RETRIEVAL SYSTEM
campus calendar, scholarships,
student and staff directories,
class openings, jobs, usernames,
tutoring schedules
TEXT -TEXT RETRIEVAL SYSTEM
campus news, encyclopedia,
computing guide, library catalog
PICT -PICTURE RETRIEVAL SYSTEM
campus and building maps, art
CAI -COMPUTER AIDED INSTRUCTION
chemistry, government, history
CTV -CABLE TV LASER DISC INSTRUCTION
logon, info, text, wps, file
WPS -WORD PROCESSING SYSTEM
spelling dictionary, thesaurus
personal publisher, file cabinet
BBS -BULLETIN BOARD SYSTEM

DESK -PERSONAL DESKTOP TOOLS
calendar, addresses, calculator
FILE -FILE PROCESSING TOOLS
edit, display, print, directory
copy, delete, watcom basic
ES -ELECTRONIC SPREADSHEET
line, bar, and pie graphs
SIGI -STUDENT CAREER GUIDANCE SYSTEM
careers, colleges, degrees
SYS -SYSTEM MANAGEMENT TOOLS
change password, help, show free
disk, ph rates, maintenance days
STAR -STUDENT TRANSCRIPTS AND RECORDS
student self pre-enrollment,
class schedule, transcript, phone
and print bill, cashiering bill
MAIL -ELECTRONIC MAIL SYSTEM
BYE -LOGOFF AND DISCONNECT

ENTER DESIRED OPTION

A menu of general applications.

show in Appendix C. Subsequently, they are issued a plastic Electronic Campus Service Card which contains their personal computer account number and a personal long distance telephone billing authorization number. Their personal computer password is shown on a removable paper backing, or carrier, affixed to each card. This card functions like a telephone calling card and is created in addition to a student's identification card because of its financial and accounting linkages. As part of the process, each student is allocated 500,000 characters of on-line disk storage on the academic timesharing cluster for general use and for an electronic mailbox.

APPLICATIONS AVAILABLE.

While categories tend to be arbitrary and fuzzy at the boundaries, the 200 timesharing computer software applications available on the Northwest Electronic Campus can be listed under at least five rubrics: software applications, database services, program languages and statistical applications, telephone services, and video services. Examples under each category are discussed.

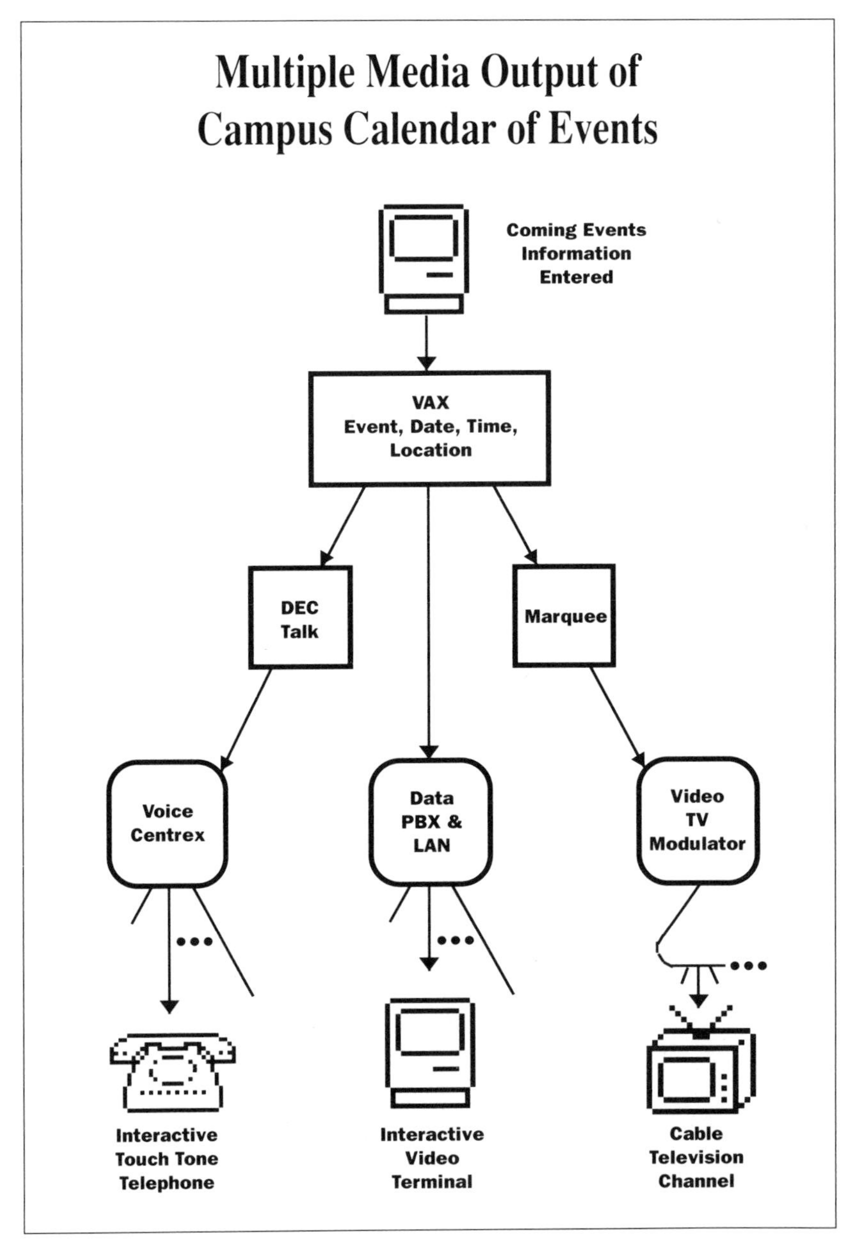
Multiple Media Output of
Campus Calendar of Events
Coming Events
Information
Entered
VAX
Event, Date, Time,
Location
DEC
Talk
Marquee
Voice
Centrex
Data
PBX &
LAN
Video
TV
Modulator
Interactive
Touch Tone
Telephone
Interactive
Video
Terminal
Cable
Television
Channel

Figure 7

Database Services. Networked on-line database services include a Reader's Guide Index service (including full abstracts), a 20-volume encyclopedia, a dictionary, thesaurus, career guidance system, and listings of University student jobs and assistantships. The Computing Services User's Guide is also on-line as shown in the main menu (pictured on page 44) of applications on the instructional computers.

With such a large array of services available in student rooms, some expressed concern that students might become hermits and never leave their rooms. As an antidote, a multimedia output system was designed for the News and Information Office through which they could distribute campus news and a calendar of up-coming events. The final form of this system, shown in Figure 7, outputs a single entry of an event through several devices: the Touch Tone Telephone retrieval system, the television marquee system and the timesharing information retrieval system accessed via keyboard. News stories written about events on

```
                  NORTHWEST - FALL 1991 CLASS SCHEDULE
                  ACADEMIC HRS - 6     ACTIVITY HRS - 0              INSTRUCTOR
DP-CRS-SC          TITLE                 CR   TIME     DAYS  BD   RM       NAME
12-130-01 USING COMPUTERS                03 0800-0850 MWF    GS  105  McDonald, Gary R
10-110-06 DEVELOPMENTAL ENGLISH          03 1200-1250 MWF    CH  347  Fry, Carrol

                  Enter a 2 to 7 digit course ID: 17-118-03          SEATS   SEATS
DP-CRS-SC  CR TITLE              TIME      DAYS  INSTRUCTOR          AVAIL   OPEN
17-118-01  3 COLLEGE ALGEBRA     0800-0850 MWF   Fuller, Jean        35      35
17-118-02  3 COLLEGE ALGEBRA     0900-0950 MWF   La Rosa, Myrna      35      35
17-118-03  3 COLLEGE ALGEBRA     1000-1050 MWF   Fink, Kurtis        24      24
17-118-04  3 COLLEGE ALGEBRA     1100-1215 TTH   Gregerson, Cher     35      35
17-118-05  3 COLLEGE ALGEBRA     1200-1250 MWF   Heintz, Christi     30      30
17-118-06  3 COLLEGE ALGEBRA     0100-0150 MWF   Heintz, Christi     30      30
17-118-07  3 COLLEGE ALGEBRA     0200-0250 MWF   Staff               30      30

Use arrow keys to scroll thru class openings; Press PF2 for HELP
PF4 to enter next course; RETURN to enroll in highlighted course
```

On-line student enrollment is simple to complete and was immediately popular with the student body. During Fall 1992 pre-registration (which took place in Spring 1991), a full 89% of students enrolled with this system, either on their own or in the offices of their academic advisors.

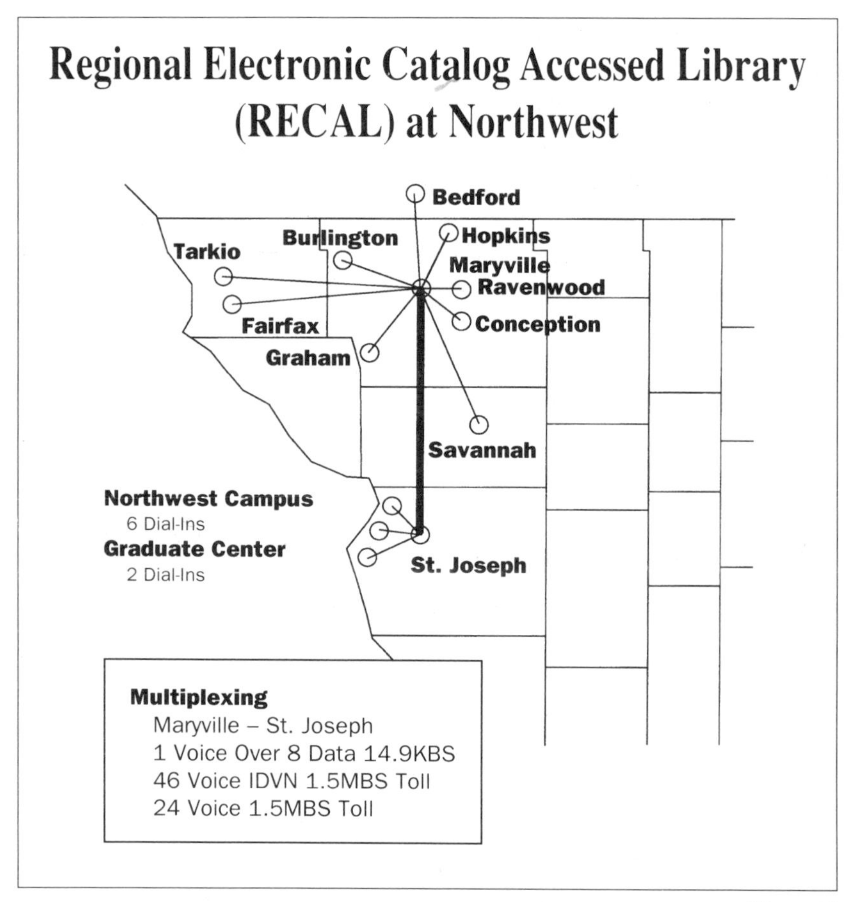

Figure 8

campus are input and are instantly retrievable on the system. This may explain why one survey found 64 percent of students using the NEWS and INFO systems.

Traversing the bureaucratic gauntlet on campus has been made easier and much faster for students using timesharing services. For example, students may self-enroll and review their class schedule, transcript and University bill from a terminal. The time required for preregistration has been reduced literally from hours to minutes. Some students report that they are now able to complete this process in as little as five minutes. When students want to preregister, they log-in to the system using their account number and retrieve a split screen display as pictured on page 46. When they select a particular course or section, they are shown how many seats are available. If they select a section with an open seat, a seat is immediately reserved for them in that section. In the upper half of the screen the system also automatically displays options of course sections when a student is unable to enroll in their first choice. The lower half of the screen shows the student's schedule as it is developed.

The library's traditional card catalog and paper files were first replaced by a computerized on-line system from OCLC (On-line Computer Library Center, Inc.) and later by a higher capacity system from Data

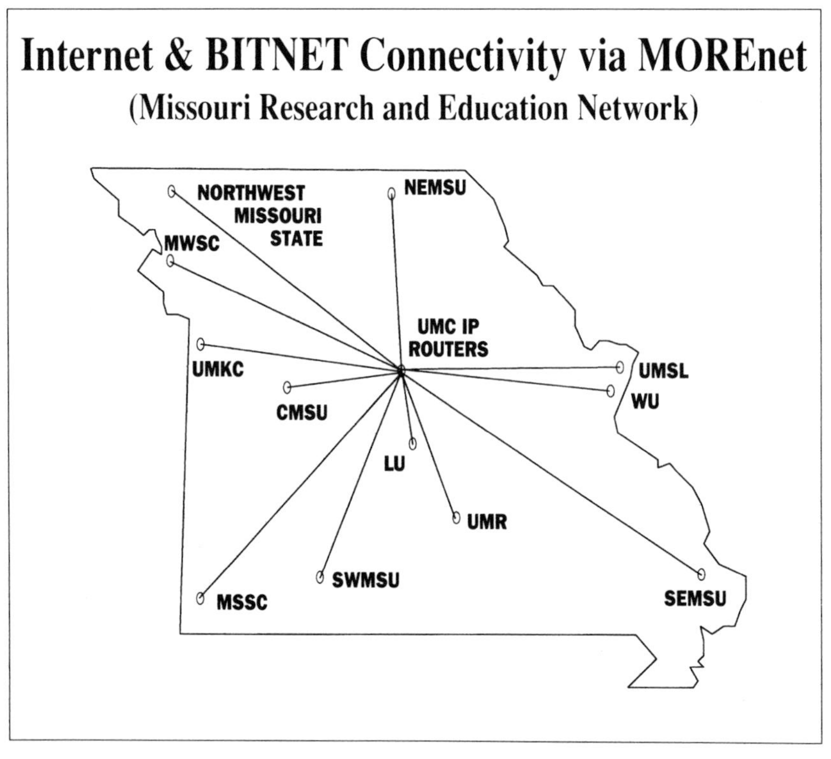

Figure 9

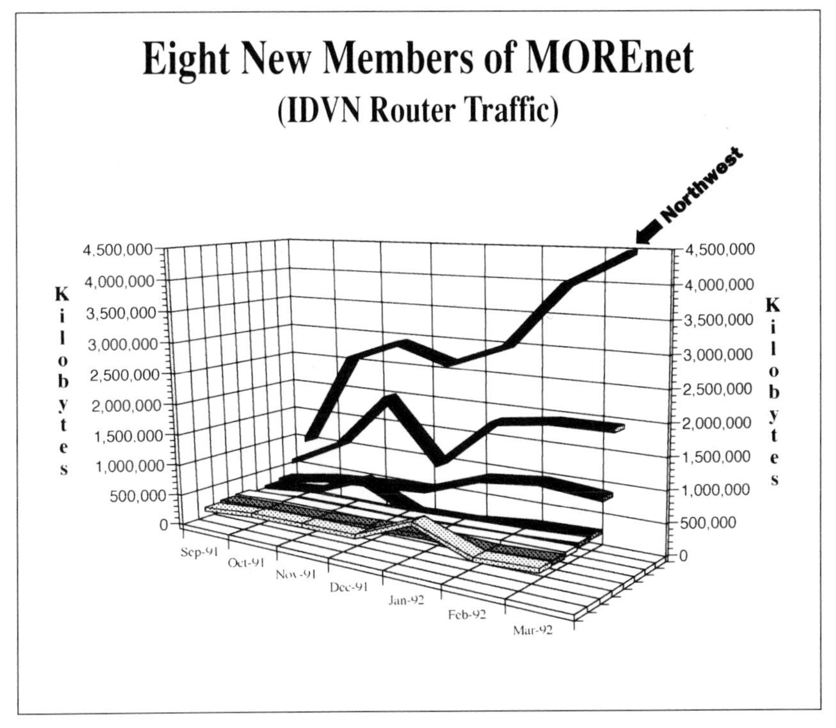

Figure 10

Research Associates, called ATLAS. The local integrated electronic catalog and circulation system was named RECAL (Regional Electronic Catalog Accessed Library). Students and faculty can quickly determine what resources are available or when they will be available, in which collection they are stored, and the appropriate call number of the item. The RECAL system permits users to search by author, book title, topic and descriptors. The system has also been made available via modems to 14 local high schools as shown in Figure 8. A courier service delivers books on a daily basis. As one high school principal put it: "Our library just went from 4,000 to 400,000 volumes!" And of course, high school students are also gaining valuable skills in library usage, along with an appreciation for the computer as a tool for retrieving remote information.

Recently, every student and faculty member has been given access

Figure 11

Compilers and Special Applications

C
BASIC
MODULA II
PROLOG
LISP
OPS5
PASCAL
COBOL
FORTRAN
ADA
Calculator
Spreadsheet
SAS
SAS Graph
Internet Telnet
Internet File Transfer

Figure 12

Touch Tone Voice Response System Menu

0 Help
1 Computing News
2 Spring Class Openings
3 Summer Class Openings
4 Fall Class Openings
5 Budget Balances
6 Campus Events Today
7 Campus Events Tomorrow
9 Voice Demonstrations
 # Restart
Restart with Menu
*** Hangup**

to Wide Area Networking via MOREnet (Missouri Research and Education network) shown in Figure 9, Missouri's gateway to world-wide Internet and BITNET services. These services include access to other Missouri state college and university library catalogs, remote databases, several remote Cray supercomputers and, of course, electronic mail. Initial MOREnet usage figures show 29,340 characters of data are transmitted per Northwest full-time equivalent student per day. Apparently 100 percent local connectivity and high access campus-wide networking paid off again since this level of activity is subtantially greater than other new members of MOREnet as shown in Figure 10.

Programming Languages and Statistical Applications. A comprehensive set of programming languages is also provided, including a statistical analysis and graphing system (see Figure 11). These services are located on a separate computer, or network node, in order to keep other nodes responsive to interactive services and requests.

Telephone Services. In addition to being able to dial the computer and receive information made intelligible by the computer's voice synthesizer, each telephone station is provided with a voice mail box with "store," "edit" and "send" functions. Message waiting notification can take three forms: (1) visually on the telephone handset; (2) audibly via a unique stutter dial tone; or, (3), when two students share a room and telephone, on a terminal monitor. Long distance billing is processed on the VAX network and provides on-line rate and billing information.

Telephone data retrieval services were available before the installation of terminals in student rooms and were very popular, but today this service is used mostly by off-campus students. However, it is still considered essential to deliver real-time, open-seat information for class enrollment by every media possible, including the telephone, since this is truly the University's most consequential consumer product. The menu of telephone retrieval services is shown in Figure 12.

Video Services. For those students with limited computer experience, Northwest uses innovative videodisc instructional programs played over cable television to instruct students regarding the system's capabilities. Northwest is a leader in the creation of such high access instructional video training systems. Video programs developed to date include step-by-step instructions on how to use the electronic library card catalog, GUEST, WPS, INFO, TEXT, PICT and STAR, in addition to other general user information systems. There are also videodiscs on campus history, a tour of the campus renewable fuel heating plant, and a tour of the computer center. In total, 144 half-hour videos can be selected from menus at terminals across campus and from any residence hall room. Any user on the system can view a menu of available videos on a terminal and select one to be played over the campus cable television network. The VAX cluster schedules showings on a first come, first serve basis for students or by requested days and times for faculty.

The Pioneer 330 Autochanger manages 8 billion frames of full motion videodiscs. Discs can be purchased for the system according to content area. For example, Northwest recently acquired a 25-platter video course on "The Mechanical Universe," and there are plans to purchase the "Twentieth Century History of the United States on Video."

Two-way video conferencing services are being added to the Northwest Electronic Campus. This compressed video service will be available in multiple buildings on campus: the conference center, the library, the student union and the Administration Building. Initial applications will focus on reducing travel costs. Given the distance to the state capital and Missouri metropolitan areas, this service is likely to have heavy use.

SUMMARY AND CONCLUSIONS.

Northwest's commitment to developing computer services as a utility for students and faculty has focused on applications which contribute to the quality of the living/learning environment, as well as to the effectiveness of the academic program. We believe that computers will increasingly be used for similar purposes in the broader society. Thus, the Northwest Electronic Campus not only represents a harbinger of things to come in America, it also prepares students to function effectively in such an environment.

5

THE IMPACT ON STUDENTS

The Northwest Electronic Campus system has now been in place since 1987 so that extensive data have been gathered regarding usage levels, growth in computer literacy, and, to a lesser extent, the impact on teaching. At the close of the 1990-91 school year the authors interviewed eight focus groups composed of from five to eight students each; a total of 60 students. Students were selected who had spent the last four years in a residence hall room equipped with a terminal, dedicated television channel and, the last two years, with a telephone. When responses from those interviews are added to the surveys which have been conducted of freshmen, several provocative and encouraging themes emerge.

CHANGING STUDENT NEEDS.

First of all, it is apparent that the cluster of applications students access will change as they progress through their academic career. All students, regardless of major or year in college, are heavy users of word processing. However, depending upon their major field of study, students branch into different applications as they progress through college. For example, business majors learn spread sheets and graphing programs while psychology majors concentrate on statistical packages. Freshmen are heavy users of E-mail; seniors reported that they used this feature less year after year. Nonetheless, seniors suggest that E-mail has important social benefits since it is "easier" to initiate social contacts over the network than in person. (One male student told of building a friendship via E-mail to the point where he and his female contact scheduled a 10 p.m. meeting under the campus' bell tower. When they arrived, 300 other students were converging on the site for the same

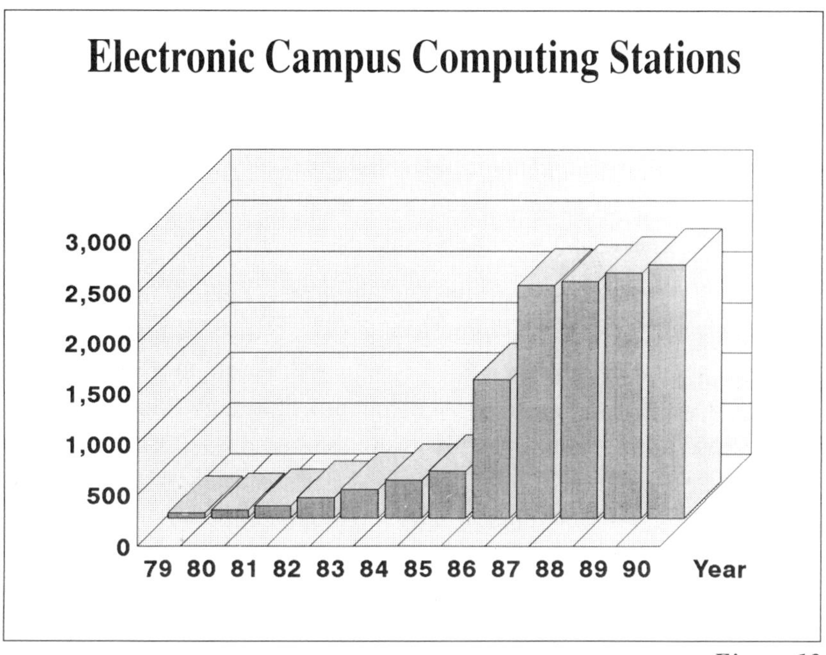

Figure 13

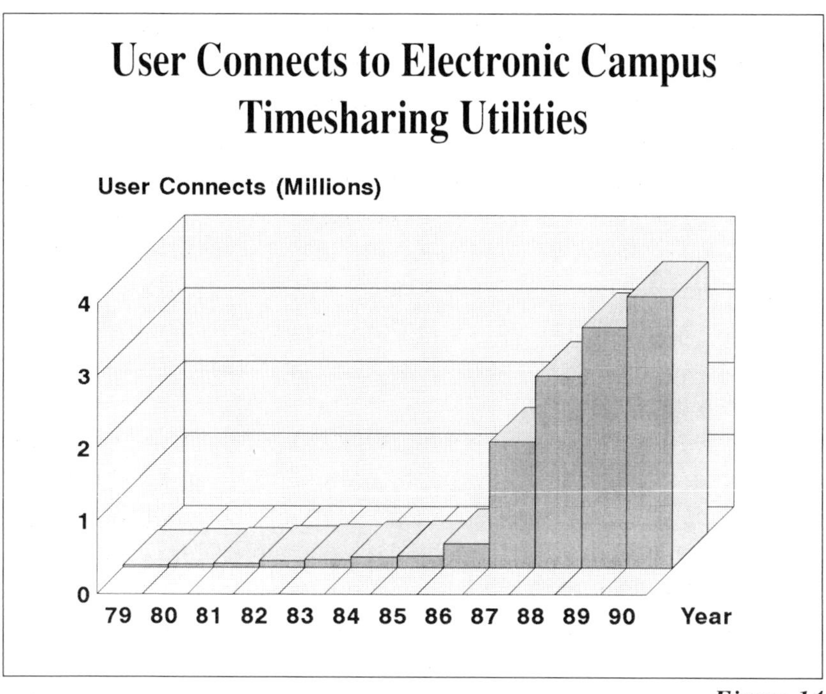

Figure 14

purpose!) There has been at least one reported marriage that resulted from an initial E-mail meeting.

When making a commitment to high access computing there is an assumption that usage will be proportional to the ease of access. The number of computing stations at Northwest, as shown in Figure 13, quadrupled in 1986 and 1987. Quantitatively, in 1990 the system processed over 100,000 "connects" from computing stations to time-sharing ports per week; about 4,000,000 per year. The number of connects for the academic years 1979 thru 1990 is shown in Figure 14. Surveys show that nearly 100 percent of residence hall occupants use the Electronic Campus an average of 8.96 hours per week; 95 percent of freshmen use word processing; 91 percent the electronic library card catalog; 82 percent electronic mail; 89 percent the directory of open class seats and the telephone directory; 64 percent read the daily news from their computer; 60 percent use the electronic encyclopedia; and 58 percent use the directory of student jobs.

There are two gross measures of system utilization: time on task, or connect time, and the number of times applications are accessed. Connect time is best to measure the utilization of applications which require large amounts of input, or keystrokes, such as word processing and text editing. The number of accesses is best to measure utilization of applications which require limited input, such as information retrieval systems or applications which perform a simple transaction. The number of accesses to popular applications is shown in Figure 15, and hours of use for input-intensive applications is shown in Figure 16.

Interestingly, 98 percent of the seniors interviewed would not pay more for a color monitor; 75 percent would not buy a notebook or microcomputer during their senior year even if the University could get them a special price.[4] (Reason: the debt load most seniors are already carrying by the time they graduate). Computer science majors seemed least interested in substituting a microcomputer for the terminal in their room. One explained, "There isn't a PC available that has the capacity and diverse languages of the VAX." Finally, all of those interviewed said they would recommend the Electronic Campus to potential freshmen; 45 percent of freshmen said the Electronic Campus was a major factor in their decision to attend Northwest (enrollment has grown 26 percent since the Electronic Campus was installed).

The impact on residence hall occupancy has also been noticeable, having grown from just under 2200 residents in 1986 to 2630 in 1991. The number of students indicating an intention to move off-campus after their freshman year has dropped 50 percent. One student who elected to move off-campus reported that "after one month I forfeited a $50 deposit on an apartment so that I could return to a residence hall with computer access."

---

[4] Hubbard, Dean; Rickman, Jon. "Northwest Missouri State University's Electronic Campus After Four Years," *THE Journal: Technological Horizons in Education*, Vol. 19, No. 3, Oct. 1991.

Access Counts of Applications for Fall Semester 1991

APPLICATION	ACCESSES
Information Retrieval Systems Campus Calendar, Class Seat Openings, Phone, V-mail and E-mail Directories, National Long Distance Rates, Jobs and Scholarships, Tutor Schedules, Career Information	**534,527**
Text Retrieval Systems Campus News, American Encyclopedia, Library Catalog, Reader's Guide, Computing Guide	**61,489**
Picture Retrieval Systems Campus Maps, Building Floor Plans, Computing Networks	**3,226**
Videodisc Retrieval System Campus, Library, Computing, Science Topics	**5,321**
Voice Retrieval and Mail Systems Messages Recorded, Messages Retrieved, Class Seat Openings, University Budget Balances	**287,102**
Student Personal Systems Self Enroll, Display Schedule, View Transcript, Show Phone and Print Usage, Display Cashier Billing	**149,270**
Faculty Personal Systems Advisees Transcripts, Test Grading, Grade Book, Purchase Orders, University Budget Balances	**8,751**

Figure 15

Following are some other interesting observations from the focus group interviews:

▼ "I never touched a computer before I came to Northwest, and now I can't live without one."

▼ "It's [the computer] my best friend."

▼ "I would have a difficult time without having access to a computer. Now I suppose I'll have to buy one when I graduate."

▼ "My brother, at another university, has to schedule a week ahead to use a PC for a half hour. My roommate and I have access to Northwest's computers from our room 160 hours per week."

▼ "When I need help on the system, I get it from other students."

▼ "As a computer science major, I like the terminal on the VAX more

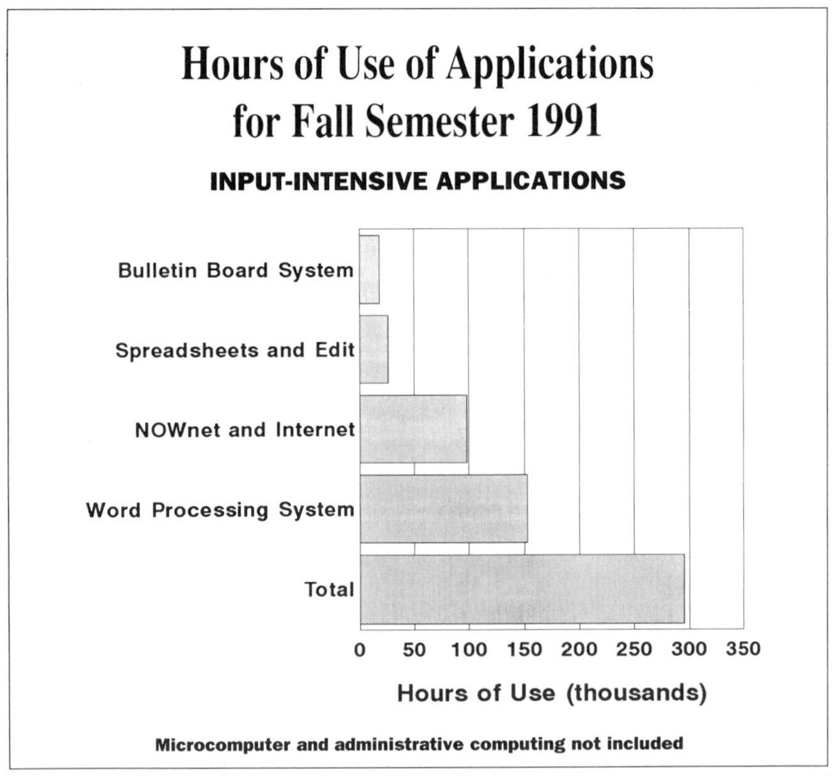

Figure 16

than a PC because it's more powerful and it's a more comprehensive system. Of course, I need *all* of the compilers."

Installing a system and keeping it operating up to user expectations for five or more years are two different challenges. A system that is easy to install may not meet a user's needs after four years of use or may not be reliable enough to count on in day-to-day situations. Once again, the graduating seniors with four years experience using the system were asked to grade the Electronic Campus on six attributes from availability and reliability to performance and friendliness. As shown in Figure 17, on a grading scale of A equals 4 to F equals 0, the seniors gave the Electronic Campus a grade point average of 3.35 with a high grade of 3.64 for providing the services and applications they needed.

Other statistics demonstrate a marked increase in the circulation

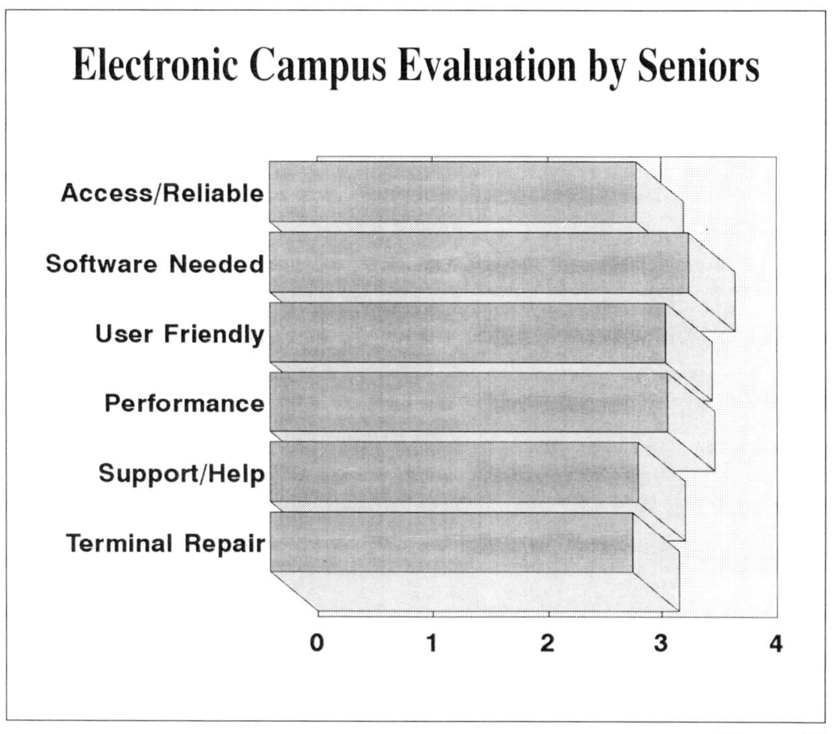

Figure 17

Even with its automated card catalog accessible to students from their residence hall rooms, traffic in Owens Library has actually increased since the Electronic Campus system was installed.

of books from the University's library as a result of the automated card catalog component of the Electronic Campus. Of course, it is impossible to tell from this data how much of the increase can be attributed to automation as opposed to automation plus access from residence hall rooms and increases in enrollment. Interestingly, contrary to what some suggested would happen when students could access the card catalog from their rooms, actual traffic in the library has increased by 34 percent during the life of the Electronic Campus. Apparently, one reason pre-Electronic Campus students were inclined to turn first to periodicals rather than books is because basic indexes are easier to use than old-fashioned card catalogs. Standard card catalog filing rules are complicated and items were sometimes misfiled alphabetically and lost in the drawers. Northwest's automated system is less threatening to students because of the variety of search techniques available. It is also more user friendly and sometimes downright fun!

A parallel study to the one conducted by the authors was carried out by two professors at Northwest which involved all graduating seniors in the class of 1990, including those living in the community. In addition to confirming the author's findings, they found 96 percent of the students rated the system as excellent (39 percent), good (48 percent) or adequate (9 percent). "Most often, students indicated their pleasure at comparing their facilities with those available to their friends from other campuses."[5] In support of high access computing, again, it was found that students who had easy access in their residence hall room to the system used it more than those who lived off campus and had to use public classroom building and library laboratories. Specifically, 100 percent of those living in residence halls used word processing compared to 80 percent of those living off-campus.

Additional enhancements completed for Northwest's automated library system include the on-line storage of 10 years of the *Reader's Guide*, accessible from any room on campus. Another improvement to the electronic card catalog is planned which will include an authority control system to refer students to correct subject headings or author entries automatically without having the student perform another search. Finally, Northwest has discovered that it is also easier to keep an electronic catalog up-to-date and make global changes with keystrokes rather than laborious hand entries.

COMPUTER USAGE AND THE RELATIONSHIP TO GRADES.

An extensive set of studies was made of E-mail usage and student academic success in the Fall of 1991.[6] Figure 18 shows the results of this study and confirms there is a relationship between lower grade point averages and excessive use of E-mail by first-time freshmen. There were 129 first-time freshmen (10.6 percent) in the residence halls who used E-mail 50 times a week or more. Of these 129 students, 37 had a semester grade point average above the campus average and 92 had a semester grade point average below the campus average. First-time freshmen living in the residence halls had an average GPA of 2.34 in the fall of 1991.

Confidentiality in this study was maintained, and students have not been tested or interviewed in an attempt to determine cause and effect.

---

[5] Thomson, Nancy S.; Chavala, Girija S. "The Electronic Campus: An Assessment," Proceedings of 1991 Decision Sciences Institute Conference, Nov. 1991, Miami Beach, Fl.

[6] Rickman, Jon; Jewell, Gabriele; Meiners, Ronald. "E-mail Usage Patterns and User Attributes." (Submitted for publication.)

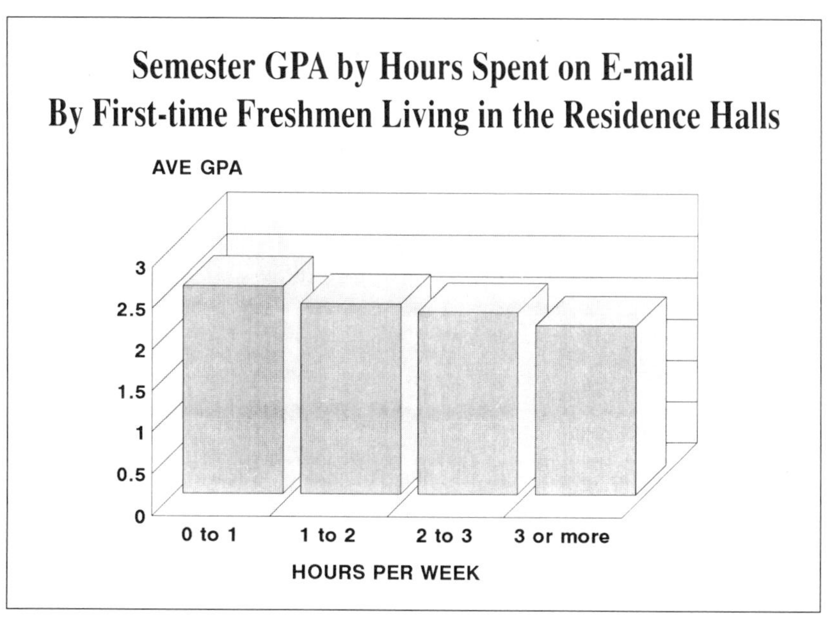

Figure 18

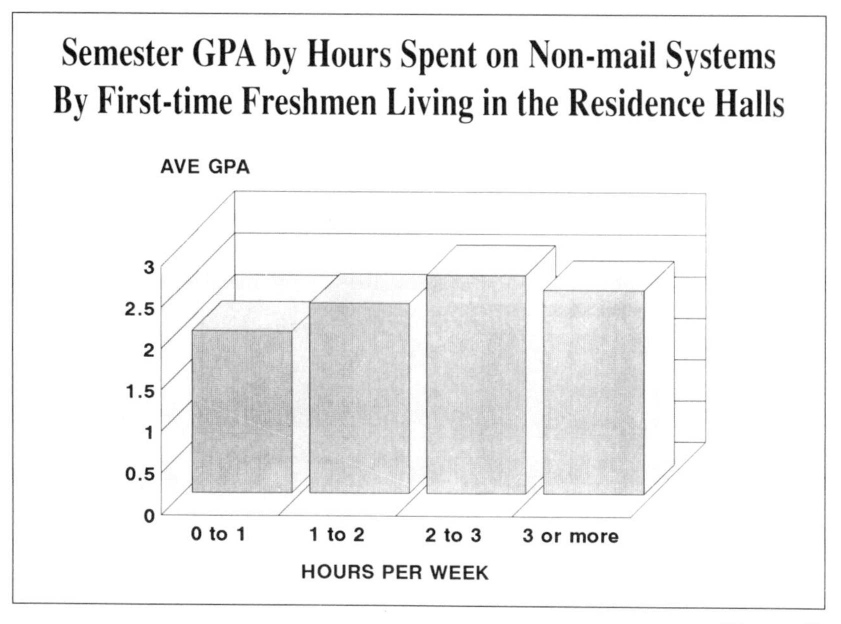

Figure 19

However, in previous years, talking to just a few confessed heavy E-mail users, one might speculate that a third factor, such as a lower level of academic motivation, could be the cause for both lower grades and excessive use of E-mail.

The study of E-mail usage in the fall of 1991 (Figure 19) also included the analysis of non-mail services. These other services were timesharing utilities, such as word processing, spreadsheets, bulletin boards, various retrieval systems, and other applications.

The analysis of the use of these other services by first-time freshmen living in the residence halls shows a trend of increasing GPAs for increased hours of usage up to three hours of use per week. For students using these other services three or more hours per week, the average GPA drops slightly; however, it remains above the average GPA for all students in the study.

In a third segment of the E-mail study it was confirmed from a survey of students that the major use of E-mail was for social purposes and E-mail had few structured academic assignments dependent on its use other than the transporting of homework. Other computing utilities on the system are applications that students primarily use as academic tools and need to complete structured academic assignments and experiences. These studies of E-mail and other services will certainly kindle more analysis and planning of appropriate or better ways to link new technologies into the multi-faceted mission of the University.

Just as a physical campus has buildings oriented to a variety of purposes (for example, a student union to meet the social needs of students and a library for their academic needs), in similar fashion the Electronic Campus has some services more oriented to social needs while others are for strictly academic needs. In both instances, student needs change as they progress toward graduation.

CURRICULUM CHANGES.

With all of the dynamics involved in the complex organization structures within a university and all the external forces affecting higher education curricula, it is very difficult to identify changes caused directly by the Electronic Campus at Northwest. It is safe to say that many courses have changed to utilize the Electronic Campus at Northwest, just as many courses have changed on other campuses in recent years due to the deployment of new computing technologies.

However, several changes in curriculum at Northwest do stand out, especially in requirements for freshmen. First-time freshmen must take a Freshman Seminar course which is integrated into a Freshman Orientation experience. These integrated experiences treat computing and electronic services on a par with the services of the library: as a provider of tools for academic endeavors. The library, in fact, employs the videodisc course retrieval system to help deliver instruction about the library to the Freshman Seminar classes. Instructors for each section of this course also spend several hours describing the services of the Electronic Campus and how students can manage their computing resources for their collegiate careers.

Every student is required to take a freshman-level "Using Computers" course. This hands-on computer literacy course uses both the timesharing utilities and desktop computing components of the Electronic Campus. Besides meeting a multitude of demands within the campus-wide curriculum, this course has also reduced the work load at the academic computing services help desk and has reduced demand for short course offerings.

Freshmen are also required to use word processing in the beginning English Composition course, and students continue to use word processing, library search systems and information retrieval systems throughout their undergraduate experience. This continued use is encouraged by the formalized Writing Across the Curriculum program at Northwest.

Writing Across the Curriculum at Northwest was spurred on by a 1984 study of student writing. Before the Electronic Campus was in place, a study was conducted by two English department faculty members which suggested that students did little writing after completing the basic general education composition requirements. That study explicitly showed on the average there were .90 major writing assign-

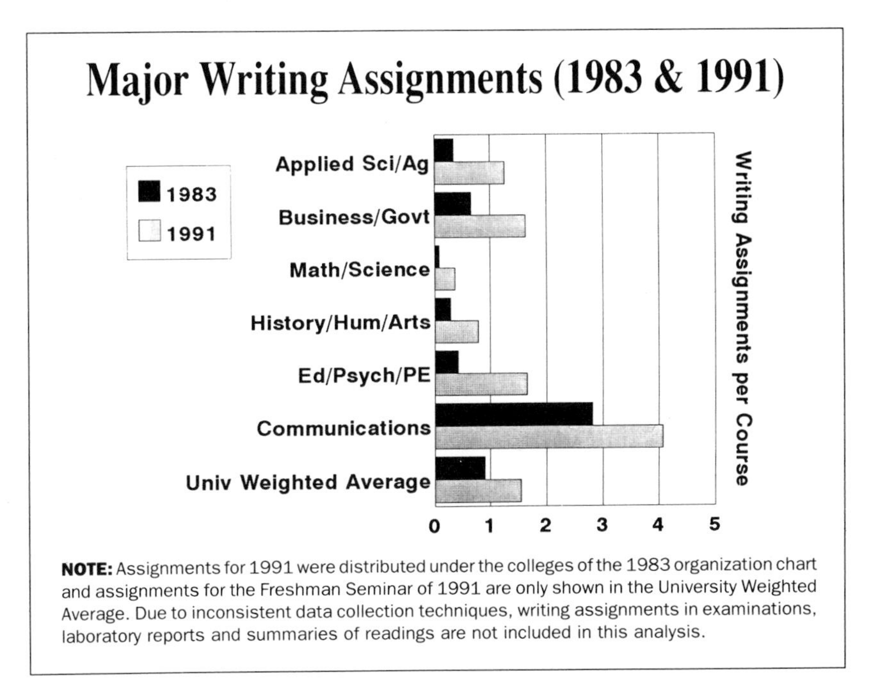

NOTE: Assignments for 1991 were distributed under the colleges of the 1983 organization chart and assignments for the Freshman Seminar of 1991 are only shown in the University Weighted Average. Due to inconsistent data collection techniques, writing assignments in examinations, laboratory reports and summaries of readings are not included in this analysis.

Table 20

ments, such as book reports, research papers and essays per course. As shown in Table 20, courses in mathematics and science had only .08 major writing assignments.

A 1992 study of the writing assignments in the fall of 1991 showed substantial increases. This study of writing assignments, made five years after the Electronic Campus was installed, revealed that students received 1.55 major writing assignments per course, for an increase of 72 percent. Table 20 shows increased major writing assignments in every college in the University, with the highest being communications at 4.07 assignments per course and the lowest being mathematics and science, which increased over four times to .37.

Total writing assignments, including major writing assignments as well as smaller ones, had reached 4.69 per course. A student with an average load of 5.77 classes was receiving 27 writing assignments per semester plus essay examinations and laboratory reports.

A recent survey of Harvard University alumni from the class of 1967 revealed the special importance of writing. When asked to rank the importance of 12 skills, 91.2 percent of the graduates ranked the skill "write effectively" as having "great importance" in their current work.[7] Quantitatively, it has been confirmed that Northwest undergraduate students must learn to write. Seniors interviewed did not view their writing assignments as burdensome because of their high access to word processing and printing facilities. Students stated that they felt that faculty members required more papers with more edits because it was easier for them to read computer-printed work than handwritten work.

SUMMARY AND CONCLUSIONS.

Northwest's Electronic Campus has exceeded expectations in every category. The level and type of usage observed suggests that Northwest students are computer-proficient as a result of having easy access to the system and are, therefore, prepared to comfortably function in an environment where computers play an increasingly important role. The system is widely used and appreciated by students and faculty, is easy to maintain and update and has had a significant impact on the academic programs of the University.

---

[7] Light, Richard J. *The Harvard Assessment Seminars*, Second Report 1992, Harvard University.

OPERATING THE SYSTEM

Two

6

TECHNICAL CONSIDERATIONS

The concept of an Electronic Campus is predicated on the expectation that all students and faculty should have convenient access to the system. Without this level of access, many of the services provided would not be effective, let alone feasible (such as electronic mail and electronic scheduling). Yet, providing thousands of input devices – whether terminals or microcomputers – is complex and expensive. The possibility for frequent malfunction and breakdown is also a major stumbling block that must be hurdled. One of the remarkable characteristics of Northwest's Electronic Campus is that it has performed almost flawlessly – at least from a user's perspective – from the day it was installed. This chapter describes the Northwest Electronic

Campus in sufficient technical detail so that other computer center directors can gain a feel for the steps involved in installing such a system.

WIRING THE CAMPUS.

Experiences with networking during the early 1980s convinced Northwest management of the enormous value and need for physically open conduits between buildings. Accordingly, six to eight large, six inch, underground conduits, containing smaller sub-conduits, were installed which connect each building on campus to a single utility tunnel. This underground conduit had an installation cost of $150,000 and is still considered one of the most valuable expenditures of the entire project. Some coax cable TV links have already been removed and replaced, some compressed video cables will be added, and even one five-year-old fiber optic cable was moved and replaced by a higher quality fiber without major campus disruptions.

At the same time, a data networking strategy was adopted which expanded two components already working on campus since 1980. One component, shown in Figure 21, was a medium-speed switched network which was designed to provide 100 percent data connectivity for all rooms on campus. The second was a high-speed computer-to-computer network, DECnet, which was later expanded to Ethernet in 1984 to connect high performance workstations. The medium speed data connectivity was designed to provide T1 multiplexed data channels through shielded jelly-filled copper cables to MICOM data switches. Voice-over-data statistical multiplexers and compressors were used to support off-campus user clusters.

In multiple computer, multiple campus, Wide Area Networking environments, a high-speed data network for each campus would be required. Each campus would need to have a very reliable backbone which reached every major building containing high power computing facilities. Any new backbone should be based on fiber optics technology for reliability.

At Northwest, the high-speed fiber optic backbone network was designed for microcomputers and VAX workstations to access multiple

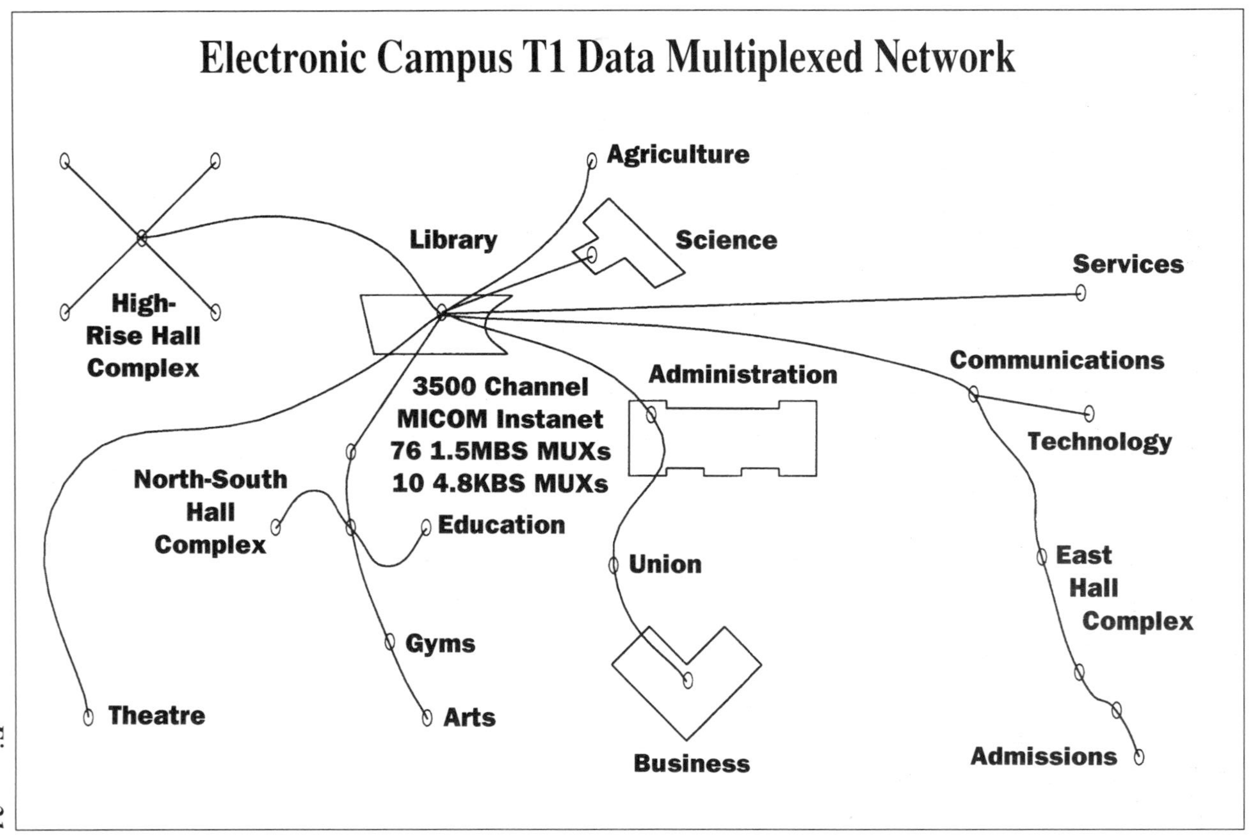
Electronic Campus T1 Data Multiplexed Network
Agriculture
Library
Science
Services
High-
Rise Hall
Complex
Communications
3500 Channel
MICOM Instanet
76 1.5MBS MUXs
10 4.8KBS MUXs
Administration
Technology
North-South
Hall
Complex
Education
Union
East
Hall
Complex
Gyms
Theatre
Arts
Business
Admissions

Figure 21

VAX timesharing computers and smaller VAX file servers and print servers. A high speed 10MBS Ethernet network of optical fiber and thinwire was designed to provide connectivity for VAXs and 32 bit microcomputers plus provide a gateway to world-wide data networks. This network (shown in Figure 22) is considered the data backbone for the Northwest campus.

An everlasting problem with large computing systems, especially those supporting non-scientific applications, is to balance input/output capacity with processing capacity. Most such systems are performance bound by their input/output capacity. Virtual memory operating systems attenuate this problem. Newly developed disk caching software systems have improved minicomputer timesharing performance as much as any single development since the advancement from swapping to paging memory management operating systems. Disk caching systems reduce real disk input reads by keeping the most recently read, or most active disk records, in main memory. If another read is initiated for these records, they are read from main memory, not the disk. Given enough memory, Northwest has experienced substantial performance improvements, as much as a factor of 10 or more, from disk caching software. Such software is an essential element in any interactive timesharing or LAN server environment.

CONFIDENTIALITY.

Data retrieval applications in an academic computing environment require special design considerations. The academic environment is famous for supporting applications under what can euphemistically be termed "friendly and unfriendly fire." Where access is desirable to selected student, administrative or even library records, one must assume some users may try hacking to gain unauthorized access. Accordingly, a desirable networking feature is to permit a large volume of student and faculty "read only" database access while providing a limited group of database custodians "read," "write" and "update" access. It is also desirable to keep unfriendly users off the computer used for maintaining records by database custodians. This is accom-

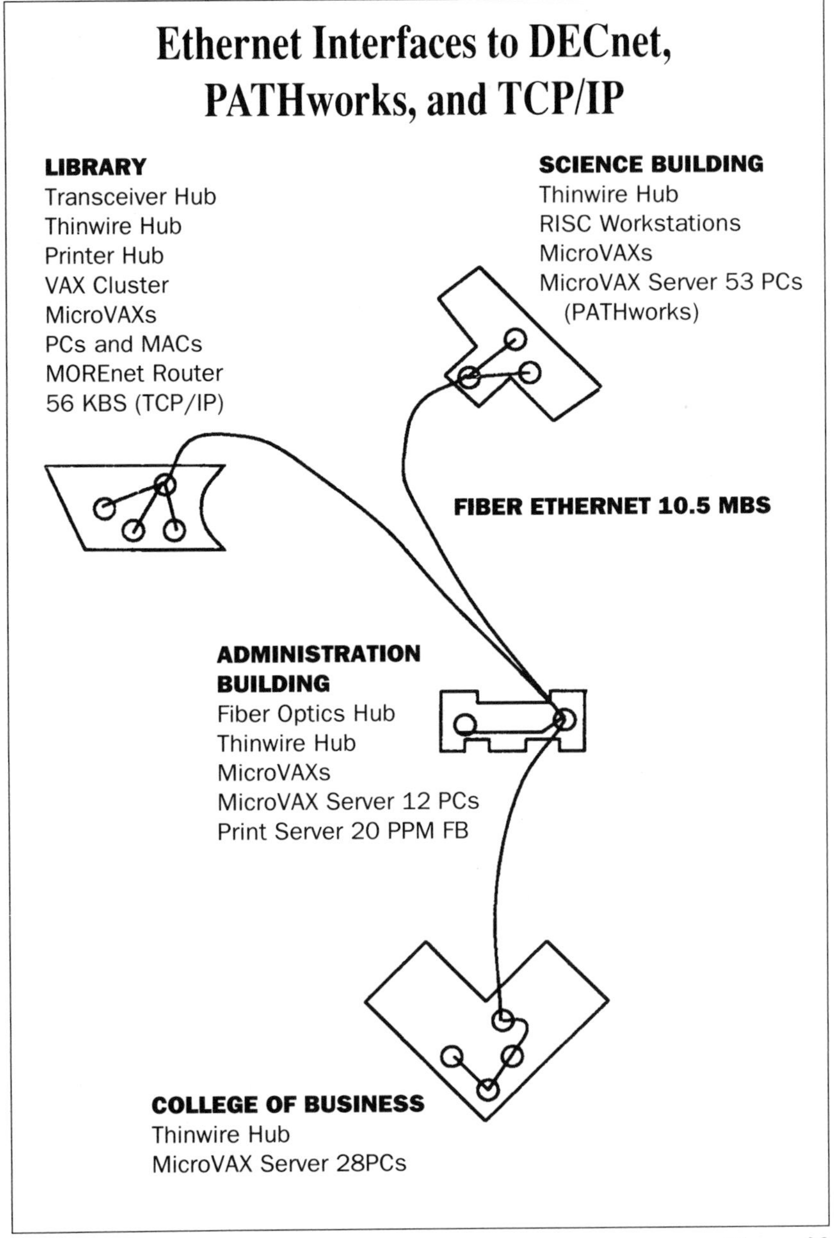
Ethernet Interfaces to DECnet, PATHworks, and TCP/IP
LIBRARY
Transceiver Hub
Thinwire Hub
Printer Hub
VAX Cluster
MicroVAXs
PCs and MACs
MOREnet Router
56 KBS (TCP/IP)
SCIENCE BUILDING
Thinwire Hub
RISC Workstations
MicroVAXs
MicroVAX Server 53 PCs
(PATHworks)
FIBER ETHERNET 10.5 MBS
ADMINISTRATION
BUILDING
Fiber Optics Hub
Thinwire Hub
MicroVAXs
MicroVAX Server 12 PCs
Print Server 20 PPM FB
COLLEGE OF BUSINESS
Thinwire Hub
MicroVAX Server 28PCs

Figure 22

plished at Northwest for some files by maintaining copies of data for user access. Copies are appropriate if they can be provided on a timely basis with respect to file change; that is, the rate of data transactions. Connecting computers to common input and output channels, or clustering computers, gives users access to shared files and is appropriate for the most rapidly changing files.

At Northwest, VAX clustering and file shadowing permits two up-to-date copies of data to be maintained simultaneously by a small computer and access by multiple large computers which allows a large number of users to read the data. Clustering at Northwest uses two high-speed file servers for multiple computers in a single computer room.

TELEPHONE SERVICES.

The telephone system at Northwest was designed to handle late evening high demand for both on- and off-campus local and long distance service. Lack of adequate local and long distance trunking has long been a serious and costly problem for many universities with PBX configurations using trunks, including Northwest. Under the old PBX system with limited residence hall access, a local trunk "all busy" signal seemed to be just part of the dial tone. The local "busy" problem was overcome on the Electronic Campus system by designing it around a Northern Telecom Centrex network which has no local campus to central office trunks. An on-site Centigram voice messaging system was added to maximize communication connects. This approach had additional appeal since it did not require extensive up-front capital funding as did the originally proposed, every room telephone PBX system (where the lowest bid was $3 million).

TELEVISION SERVICES.

Today, most students expect at least some television service in their living quarters. At Northwest, traditional radio and television satellite receivers, broadcasting systems, camera studios and editing laboratories augment automated Electronic Campus television channels. Television services are delivered over a standard coax cable network. Instructional video is stored on a Pioneer, digitally controlled, 72-platter

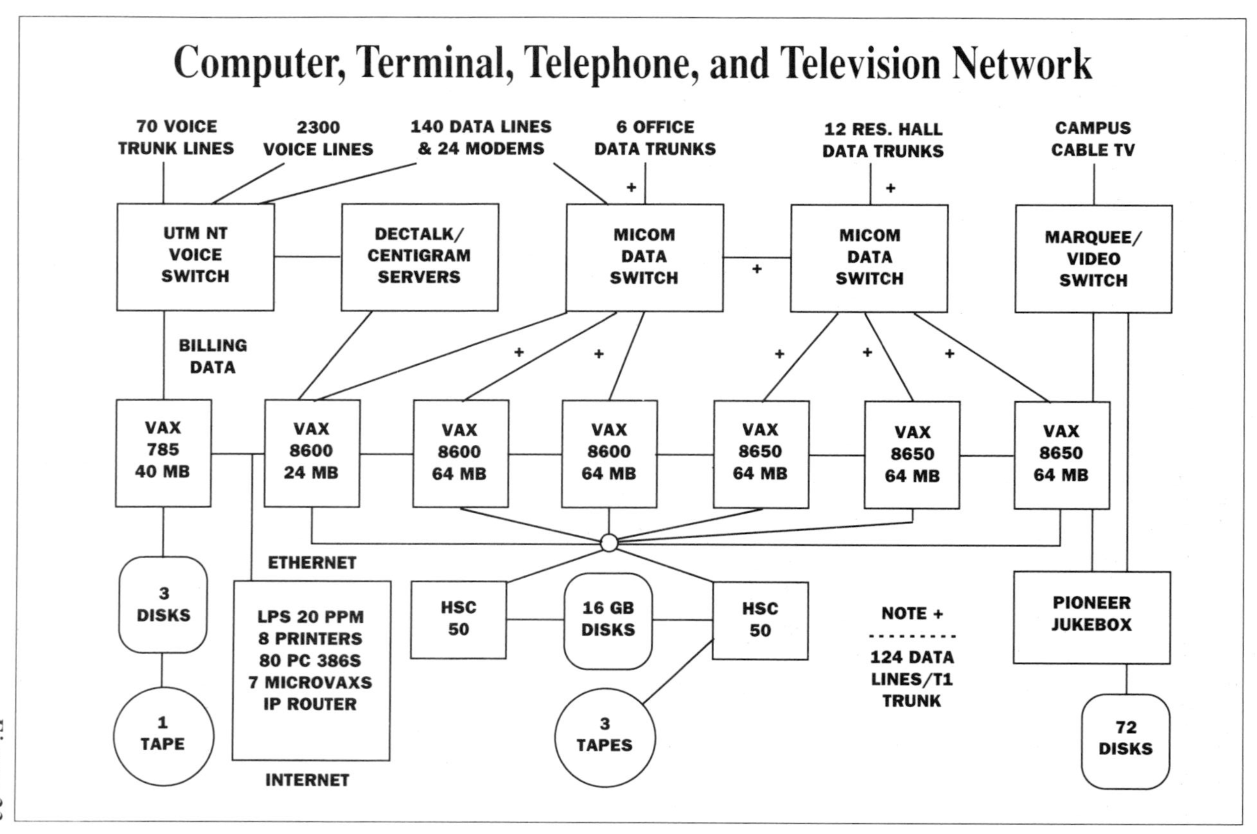
Computer, Terminal, Telephone, and Television Network
70 VOICE TRUNK LINES
2300 VOICE LINES
140 DATA LINES & 24 MODEMS
6 OFFICE DATA TRUNKS
+
12 RES. HALL DATA TRUNKS
+
CAMPUS CABLE TV
UTM NT VOICE SWITCH
DECTALK/ CENTIGRAM SERVERS
MICOM DATA SWITCH
+
MICOM DATA SWITCH
MARQUEE/ VIDEO SWITCH
BILLING DATA
+
+
+
+
+
VAX 785 40 MB
VAX 8600 24 MB
VAX 8600 64 MB
VAX 8600 64 MB
VAX 8650 64 MB
VAX 8650 64 MB
VAX 8650 64 MB
ETHERNET
3 DISKS
LPS 20 PPM
8 PRINTERS
80 PC 386S
7 MICROVAXS
IP ROUTER
HSC 50
16 GB DISKS
HSC 50
NOTE +
124 DATA LINES/T1 TRUNK
PIONEER JUKEBOX
1 TAPE
INTERNET
3 TAPES
72 DISKS

Figure 23

videodisc jukebox. A video switch is used, which is also digitally controlled, to feed the calendar of events marquee or the videodisc to the distribution modulator. Figure 23 shows the MICOM data, Ethernet data, telephone and television networks for the Northwest Electronic Campus.

SUMMARY AND CONCLUSIONS.

Northwest Missouri State University has demonstrated that the technical challenges associated with providing extensive access to computer services can be overcome on a mid-sized university campus. In order to ensure flexibility and ease of upgrading, an adequate system of conduit linking all parts of the campus is essential. By judiciously allocating low- and high-speed connections to the system, resources can be stretched to provide everyone with convenient network access. Additionally, this can be done at a reasonable cost.

7

MAINTAINING THE SYSTEM

Maintenance is an important factor that must be considered when designing a computer system. Consideration should extend beyond keeping the hardware running to include all responsibilities typically assigned to a computer center staff such as training, vendor relations, purchasing, maintaining an inventory of spare parts and software support. Regardless of which metric is used for comparison, Northwest's system has proved to be remarkably efficient. This chapter outlines the approach used to keep the system in operation for over five years with a staff of only 15 full-time employees plus part-time student employees.

MAINTENANCE PHILOSOPHY.

Northwest's Electronic Campus maintenance strategy keys off a simple dictum: restrict variation in hardware and software. If the "support plane" as well as the "support volume" can be controlled, then it is much easier to control the cost of support. An idealized "support volume" can be visualized as a three dimensional space where the number of hardware platforms and the number of software packages are shown on the x and y axes of a plane, while the number of users are shown on the vertical z axis. Support volume is the product of these three components as shown in Figure 24.

The number of users of a computing network is the most interesting component of support volume. The typical college or university wants to maximize, not restrict, the number of users. At first glance, it seems apparent that if access to computing is increased until the number of computing stations approaches the number of users, then the variable "users" can be replaced by the variable "stations." However, this would

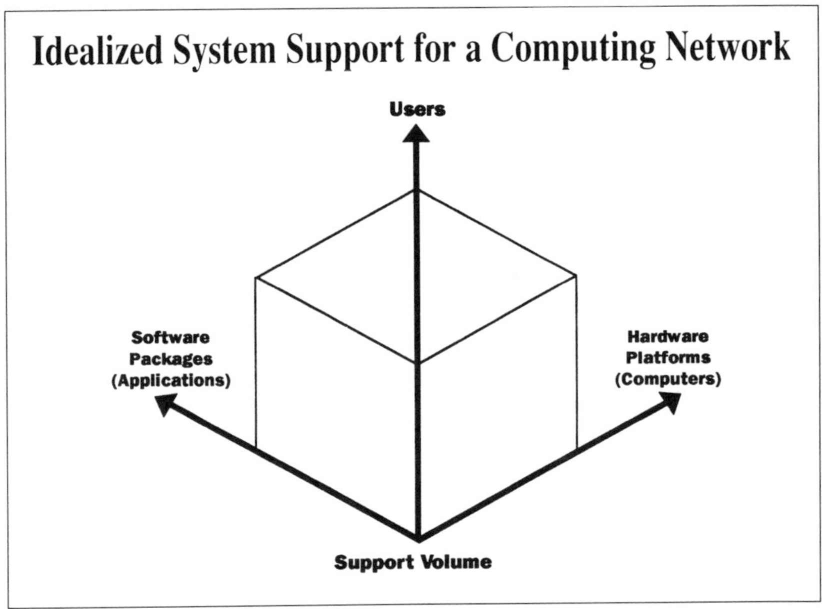

Figure 24

not completely describe an equivalent variable in support volume since the "users" component also encompasses both training issues and problem resolution support. Therefore, we will stay with the number of users as the vertical component of the support volume. It should be kept in mind that if a system can be designed which minimizes the time spent keeping machines running, then obviously more time can be spent training and supporting users, the reason the system exists in the first place.

Northwest's department of Computing Services and Telecommunications is made up of 15 full-time professional staff and a dozen or more part-time student workers. As shown in the organization chart in Figure 25, the staff is responsible for all computing and telecommunications (telephone plus compressed and cable television) hardware plus all timesharing, networking, and telecommunications software management. The size of the full-time staff has not been increased even though the number of stations has been quadrupled; in fact, the staff is smaller than that of many smaller institutions. The staff is less than one fourth the size of just the Computing Services Department of a similar-sized private institution which requires its students to purchase their own microcomputers.

Administrative departments are responsible and accountable for the input and management of all the data associated with their departments. Academic departments are responsible for software and user support of their microcomputer laboratories.

CONTROLLING PURCHASES.

Controlling the variety of machines and software applications purchased is particularly difficult (sometimes impossible) in state institutions which require open bidding. In such settings it is not uncommon for the vendor with which an institution must do business to change annually from one bid to the next or from contract to contract. Even when this is not a problem, new models and new versions eclipse old models and versions, adding to the variation with which support staffs must cope. Even a variation in main memory sizes or disk drive

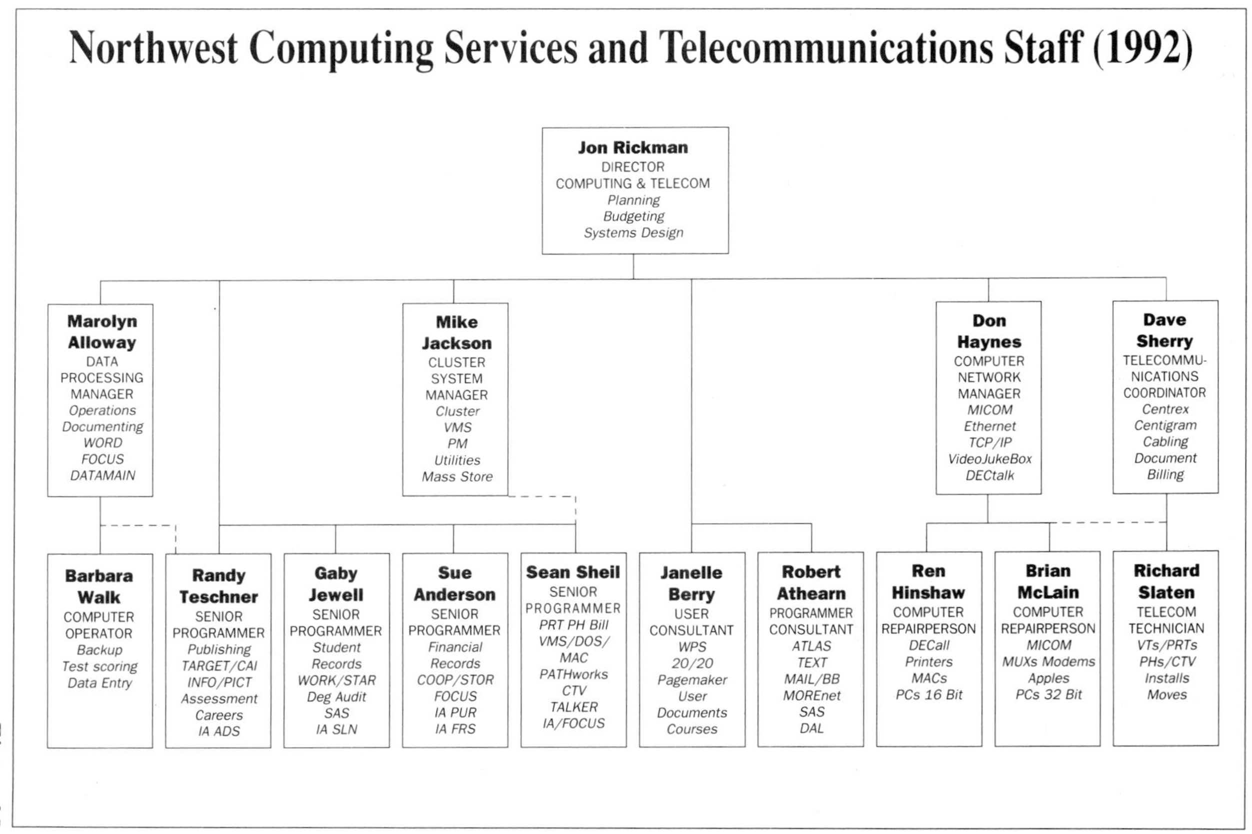
Northwest Computing Services and Telecommunications Staff (1992)
Jon Rickman
DIRECTOR
COMPUTING & TELECOM
Planning
Budgeting
Systems Design
Marolyn Alloway
DATA PROCESSING MANAGER
Operations
Documenting
WORD
FOCUS
DATAMAIN
Mike Jackson
CLUSTER SYSTEM MANAGER
Cluster
VMS
PM
Utilities
Mass Store
Don Haynes
COMPUTER NETWORK MANAGER
MICOM
Ethernet
TCP/IP
VideoJukeBox
DECtalk
Dave Sherry
TELECOMMUNICATIONS COORDINATOR
Centrex
Centigram
Cabling
Document
Billing
Barbara Walk
COMPUTER OPERATOR
Backup
Test scoring
Data Entry
Randy Teschner
SENIOR PROGRAMMER
Publishing
TARGET/CAI
INFO/PICT
Assessment
Careers
IA ADS
Gaby Jewell
SENIOR PROGRAMMER
Student
Records
WORK/STAR
Deg Audit
SAS
IA SLN
Sue Anderson
SENIOR PROGRAMMER
Financial
Records
COOP/STOR
FOCUS
IA PUR
IA FRS
Sean Sheil
SENIOR PROGRAMMER
PRT PH Bill
VMS/DOS/
MAC
PATHworks
CTV
TALKER
IA/FOCUS
Janelle Berry
USER CONSULTANT
WPS
20/20
Pagemaker
User
Documents
Courses
Robert Athearn
PROGRAMMER CONSULTANT
ATLAS
TEXT
MAIL/BB
MOREnet
SAS
DAL
Ren Hinshaw
COMPUTER REPAIRPERSON
DECall
Printers
MACs
PCs 16 Bit
Brian McLain
COMPUTER REPAIRPERSON
MICOM
MUXs Modems
Apples
PCs 32 Bit
Richard Slaten
TELECOM TECHNICIAN
VTs/PRTs
PHs/CTV
Installs
Moves

Figure 25

sizes can greatly increase the number of support problems to be solved in a large network of microcomputers. Likewise, any variation in versions or revisions of software products can also increase the number of support problems. Northwest has sought to minimize these problems by batching acquisitions together in order to acquire as many similar items as possible in each purchase.

Complicating matters even further is the practice of allowing users essentially to vote on what software will be supported on the system. For example, if microcomputer word processing packages are chosen because of current popularity alone and not function, then history suggests that the application supported will change every two or three years. (For example, in the mid 1980s Word Star was the biggest seller nationally, then WordPerfect dominated the market, and now it is being challenged by Microsoft Word.) At Northwest we have been able to resist this tendency by reminding each other that the goal is to teach computing, not a specific software package. Interestingly, students have been less likely than faculty and staff to lobby for the most currently popular software.

While Northwest has been able to control the variety of different hardware platforms which can be purchased by requiring that the director of computing services approve purchases, it is not as easy or maybe even desirable to exercise the same rigid control over software packages. However, that does not mean that support staff should be expected to support esoteric applications. Northwest annually defines in its User's Guide a subset of applications which will be eligible for campus-wide support services. Those choosing applications not on the supported list are asked to find help elsewhere or to contract from their operating budgets for services from the vendor. Since the subset includes products with a wide range of functionality, most users check the list of supported items before making purchases.

HARDWARE MAINTENANCE.

At Northwest, maintenance of computer terminals is handled the same as telephones. The fact that terminals do not contain disk drives makes it possible for a single crew of students to quickly swap out broken units without concern for floppy disk drive alignment or hard disk data security, a problem they could confront if they were servicing microcomputers. On the same repair rounds, they also swap out faulty telephone cords or handsets and even faulty television cable jacks. Experience has shown that equipment in residence hall rooms requires more maintenance than similar equipment in offices. This is partly due to multiple users in the residence hall room and sometimes very crowded conditions.

Maintenance is only one of the reasons Northwest chose not to place or support microcomputers in residence halls. There is also the vexing problem of unauthorized copying of software. Additionally, problems related to uniform training and addiction to computer games are minimized with a common timesharing system. When microcomputers are located in supervised laboratories, especially next to faculty offices, these and similar problems can be better addressed.

The most challenging upper management task with timesharing systems is to ensure good response times by keeping the timesharing power growth curve ahead of the demand curve. Management can delay the demand curve by limiting or restricting the number of simultaneous log-ins only for a short period of time. The microcomputer analog of this management challenge is trying to fund additional microcomputers and networking ahead of the demand curve. At state supported comprehensive universities this can limit potential new users for a long, long period of time.

SOFTWARE SUPPORT.

In a university environment, the number of different software packages can become very large even if the number of vendors of similar packages is restricted. Obviously, the potential for unique applications within the diverse curriculum of a modern university is enormous. One strategy to survive this situation is to organize support based on the 80-20 percent rule. That is, assume 80 percent of the users need 20 percent of the applications while 20 percent of the users need 80 percent of the applications. Thus, a central support staff can be trained and assigned to support a limited number of software applications for the majority of users. Studies show that this set of users will need support for word processing, electronic mail, electronic spreadsheets and retrieval services, or the applications we have come to call "utilities." Figure 26 shows this support volume for 80 percent of the users on a restricted support plane.

Keeping a limited number of hardware platforms and software products for these users is very important to improve peer support. As a counter example, consider how little technical help a dedicated user of a Macintosh running Microsoft Word can expect to receive from a user of an MS-DOS computer running WordPerfect. It's discouraging, but true.

For the other 20 percent of the users who use 80 percent of the total applications, centralized support is difficult, if not impossible.

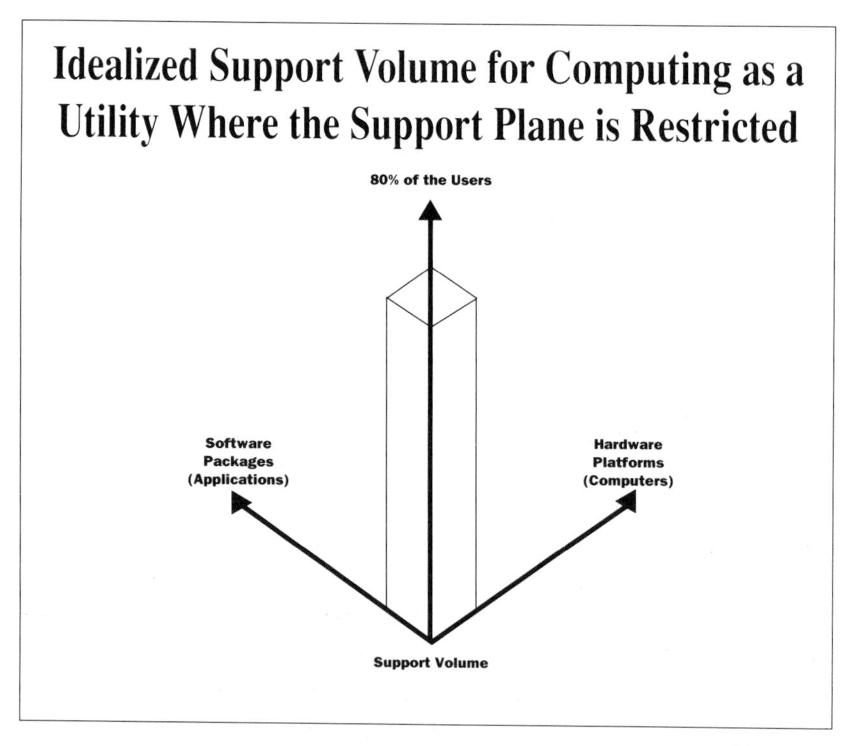

Figure 26

Northwest's strategy has been to distribute software applications required by this small group across campus to departmental laboratories with localized support. Support may come from the professor if his or her students are the only users of an application. This situation can be represented as a support plane broken by application software packages as shown in Figure 27 where specialized application laboratories are distributed across campus. Note that pursuing this model permits an institution to allow diversity while restricting hardware platform variations in order to provide cost-efficient centralized hardware repair and support.

ENVIRONMENTAL PROBLEMS.

Northwest soon discovered that hidden villains lurked in many student rooms. Heavy current-drawing electrical appliances are everywhere: hair dryers, curling irons, irons, stereos, you name it, all plugged into one or two outlets! Therefore, the fewer costly electronics physically in the room, the better. For maintenance reasons alone, it is better not

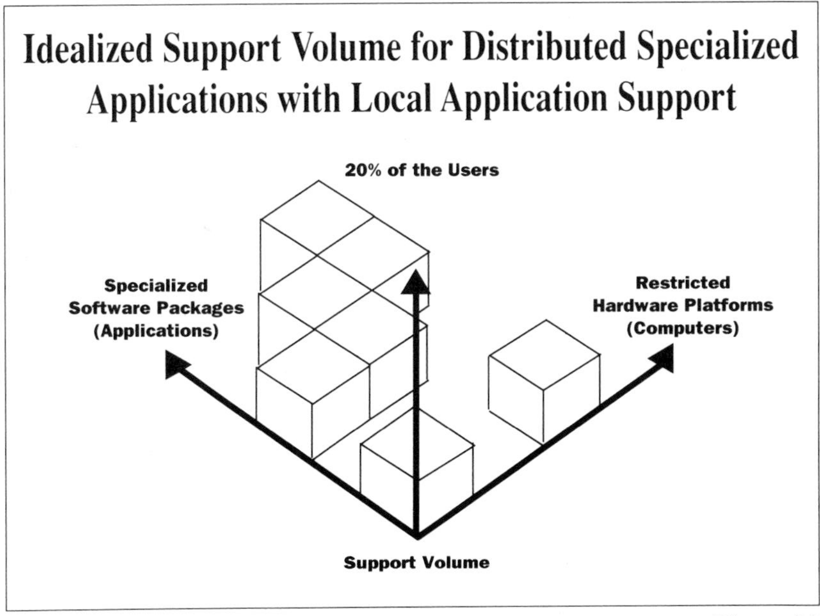

Figure 27

to have disk drives, mother boards and expensive LAN interface boards in students' residence hall rooms. Considering maintenance and security issues only, one might describe the ideal computing station for a university residence hall room as one with zero disk drives, zero memory, zero processors and zero street value; i.e., a terminal.

Finally, a word about lightning strikes seems appropriate since most schools are forced to locate at least some computer equipment in old and poorly wired buildings. After losing terminals in the Administration Building (constructed before 1910) to a lightning storm, Northwest formed a task force to resolve the problem. Even though other buildings on campus were taller and it seemed that they would provide better targets for lightning strikes, lightning rods were installed on the tall, commanding turret towers of the Administration Building. Nonetheless, the Administration Building continued to suffer lightning strikes, and terminals continued to be damaged. Finally, the task force found that the neutral-to-ground strap was missing at the main power entrance in the basement. With the grounding strap now in place the old campus landmark has become a lot friendlier to high-tech electronics. The obvious lesson: carefully check every aspect of the wiring in old buildings before installing computers or even terminals.

SHARING RESOURCES.

When resources are shared by students, or by anyone for that matter, maintenance problems can increase dramatically. The same equipment that disintegrates in a student lounge may last for years and years in a private office or residence hall room which requires a damage deposit. Less obvious are problems associated in sharing permanent disk storage and software. The experience at Northwest suggests that the software maintenance problems in a computing network are proportional to the number of hard disks and/or the number of software operating systems. Many microcomputer operating systems, especially MS-DOS, permit accidental or unfriendly access and erasure of data and even crucial system files such as the AUTOEXEC.BAT file or the CONFIG.SYS file. After all, a personal computer was designed to be a private personal resource, not a shared resource. In addition to file corruption, other problems exist, such as no one wanting the responsiblity to back up the hard disk storage. It should be remembered that on a college or university campus most resources need to be shared, even in a residence hall room.

The primary goal of LAN development in the last 10 years has been to make personal computers sharable and able to share other computing resources. It again appears that the fewer number of LAN servers with hard disks one has to support in a network, the more efficient LAN maintenance can be implemented. In the same way Northwest has chosen data and voice network technology, Northwest has again chosen a LAN technology with the capacity to serve the entire campus and not just one department or one building. If one would not consider an intercom telephone system for one building why would one want to consider a LAN which will reach its maximum capacity in one laboratory or building?

SUMMARY AND CONCLUSIONS.

In summary, the good news is that Northwest's experience shows that if hardware and software variations are controlled, the support load on a service center is not directly proportional to the number of users. When most users are using similar hardware and software and there is a high density of computing stations, then every fellow student, colleague or peer becomes a potential resource for support.

Northwest Missouri State University has demonstrated that an extensive, comprehensive computing system can be provided to a diverse group of users without encountering heavy maintenance costs. Achieving this ideal has required sharply focused goals and a disciplined approach to acquisitions.

SECURING THE FUTURE

Three

8

WHERE DO WE GO FROM HERE?

The Northwest Electronic Campus has stood the test of time and experience. It has been in operation since 1987 and has positively impacted teaching, learning and the general campus environment. Northwest graduates and Northwest students are unquestionably computer literate and computer proficient as a result of having easy access to the system and are, therefore, prepared to comfortably function in an environment where computers play an increasingly important role. This innovation has exceeded expectations in nearly every category. It is widely used and appreciated by students and faculty. A small staff has been able to maintain and update the system. Further, it allows the University the flexibility necessary to remain at the cutting edge of this rapidly evolving field.

FUTURE THRUSTS.

During the summer of 1992, Northwest increased its timesharing and network server computing power to almost 100 MIPS (Million Instructions Per Second) in order to keep its computing power supply ahead of demand. Two VAX 6610 computers, each with 32 MIPS of processing power, four VAX 4000 computers, and RISC computers replaced several VAX 8000 machines. The entire upgrade was accomplished in a few weeks at a cost of only $15 per semester per student over the next five years, including maintenance. In all, this network upgrade was dedicated to the Electronic Campus services which one

Computers play an increasingly important role in every student's classroom experience at Northwest.

might consider above and beyond the services expected or required at any institution and represent the major ongoing computer costs of the Electronic Campus. This newest computer network configuration is shown in Appendix D.

After visitors to campus have had a thorough orientation to the system, the most frequently asked question is: What comes next? Where does Northwest Missouri State University plan to go from here in the area of computing? The answer to these and similar questions is shaped in part by our expectations regarding where computing in general is headed. It should be pointed out that the graduating seniors in the focused interview groups did not expect the menu of services for the Electronic Campus to be expanded to any great extent. Of those interviewed, 98 percent believed the terminal in their room was worth the $25 charge built into their room fees. But if it were to cost more money, the only upgrade they were interested in was to have more printers available for student rental. Even here, only 50 percent agreed that they would have paid $20 more to have a printer.

A cursory review of the literature suggests that many view timesharing computer systems as on the way out to be replaced by microcomputers networked together through Local Area Networks. In *Life After Television*, George Gilder even goes so far as to suggest that the advent of the "telecomputer" will render databases along with LANs obsolete by giving local users instant access to massive databases.[8] He doesn't suggest who will maintain the integrity of all these data. On the other hand, some telephone company representatives envision a day when subscribers will rent the use of software and storage space on huge timesharing computers ("big hummers") housed in telephone company offices. According to this scenario, why would anyone want or need a microcomputer?

As far as colleges and universities are concerned, in the Summer 1991 issue of *EDUCOM Review*, Kenneth Green and Skip Eastman

---

[8] Gilder, George. *Life After Television: The Coming Transformation of Media and American Life.* Whittle Direct Books, 1990.

suggest that students will increasingly be expected to purchase their own computers, even as they are usually expected to buy their own textbooks.[9] The one clear theme that emerges from this cacophony of prognostication is that educational institutions need systems which can be easily adapted to fit an ongoing dizzying stream of innovations in the field of computing.

PROJECTING THE FUTURE.

While we don't have any better grasp of the future than anyone else (after all, it's difficult to prophecy, especially about the future!), Northwest's current plans are based upon the following assumptions:

1. Ease of access and the cost of computer services increasingly will be an important factor in students' choices of where to go to college.

2. Students and faculty will increasingly expect the computer to be treated like any other utility on campus. In other words, they will expect convenient and free access to computer resources and expect to be able to access information which will compliment their educational tasks.

3. The microcomputer is an interim technology which is even now being merged into the notebook computer. As low cost color screens become available for these machines there will be diminished reasons to purchase a desktop microcomputer.

4. Within the decade the predominant mode of computing on campus will be notebook computers which can easily be connected through ubiquitous outlets to large powerful networks of computers permitting the sharing of nearly any imaginable digitized resource.

5. The next generation of timesharing computers will be able to support applications from multiple operating systems including

---

[9] Green, Kenneth C. and Eastman, Skip. "Access to Computing: How Many Computers and Where Do We Put Them," *EDUCOM Review*, Vol. 26, No. 2, Summer 1991, p. 61.

UNIX, VMS and Windows. They will be much more powerful and less expensive than today's machines.

6. Eventually, differences between computers and TV sets will disappear in the face of digital electronics. "Telecomputers" will greatly facilitate accessing remote databases for a host of applications. These devices, whatever they are called, will perform dual functions. Not only will the same monitor be used to watch TV, communicate with compressed video and perform normal computing functions, it will do all three simultaneously. (One will be able to write an article while watching a ball game in a window, the size of which can be controlled. Also, the action can be digitally recorded, allowing for custom replays!)

7. With usage increasing dramatically in all segments of society, the computer will join telephone and energy systems as an expected utility in every organization.

In light of these assumptions, Northwest will continue to incrementally develop and deliver comprehensive utilitarian electronic services to everyone on campus with multimedia communications, including compressed video. Other on-campus possibilities include compressed video tutoring employing windowing on terminals and microcomputers. Multimedia laboratories supporting compressed digitized video, digitized voice, and data applications could also be developed to enhance the delivery of instruction orginating at remote sites or the delivery of instruction to high school teachers in our region.

In the future Northwest hopes to expand its focus to include developing specialized electronic services for off-campus learners. For example, along with extending MOREnet services to regional school districts, applications of notebook computers and digital cellular towers can hopefully be studied. Taking a new direction from past themes of connnectivity and providing a comprehensive set of tools for the University environment, the Electronic Campus could be expanded to include several high-tech "Computer Simulated Experience" centers targeted on area school children. These centers would be designed to motivate students to study science and mathematics.

Northwest is also considering other ComSE (pronounced "Come See") computer simulated experience centers in the areas of mathematics and science. Others could be for the promotion of learning in the areas of farming, food production and environmental studies. In this center students would use computers to simulate plant growth, erosion, water supply, air quality, by-product energy development, food production, recycling, water management and population food demand.

Another center could focus on tele-conferencing, business writing and composition, electronic and voice mail, compound interest models, supply and demand pricing models, robotics and labor costing models, currency exchange simulation, tariff and tax modeling, and stock exchange simulation.

All of the ComSE centers would involve heavy use of computer simulations to excite and stimulate student desire for an understanding of real-world problems and appreciate the need to develop the skills necessary to solve these problems. While all of the above are still in the "blue-sky" stage of development and will require funding, additional staff, and several years to complete, they illustrate new ways in which the Electronic Campus may be extended for the local communities in the future.

TOWARD BUILDING AN AGENDA FOR THOSE CONTEMPLATING AN ELECTRONIC CAMPUS.

The following list reflects what we've learned over the past 14 years as the Electronic Campus was evolving at Northwest Missouri State University.

Focus and Balance. What can be said of any other activity is also true of computing: Very little that is meaningful takes place in an unstructured environment. Clear goals and objectives are primary mechanisms for creating structure. Therefore, the first issue which must be decided in planning a campus computer system is, "What will its focus be?"

Infrastructure. Second, an infrastructure must be designed within physical constraints which will facilitate innovation and change. There is nothing more unsightly – or costly – than keeping a campus torn up with trenches for new cabling projects.

Hardware. An economical approach to hardware will greatly simplify maintenance, networking, training and general system development. Expensive and/or complex systems which are difficult to maintain should be physically isolated and protected from unfriendly or naive users. Finally, the institution should decide on a vendor and stick with it.

Software. A frugal approach should also be taken to software. Consideration should be given to whether or not the operating system software can protect its most complex components from tampering by naive, malicious or mischievous users.

Training. Begin with faculty, automate as much as possible and repeat frequently. Also, have moderate expectations regarding the size group which constitutes a "successful" session.

SUMMARY AND CONCLUSIONS.

To us it seems obvious that today's college graduate must be computer proficient in order to function effectively in our rapidly changing society. How to provide adequate equipment so that students can develop such proficiency is a major challenge confronting post-secondary institutions today. When the average institution is able to provide only one computing station for every 47.3 undergraduate students, then surely a better model needs to be found.[10] We believe Northwest's Electronic Campus, which provides a universal telephone and computing service with one computing station for every 2.8 undergraduate students, represents such a viable, low-cost model which meets the current needs of faculty and students while providing the flexibility necessary to move with the cutting edge of this rapidly evolving field.[11]

---

[10] Green, Kenneth C. and Eastman, Skip. "Access to Computing: How Many Computers and Where Do We Put Them," *EDUCOM Review*, Vol. 26, No. 2, Summer 1991, p. 59.

[11] "Universal Telephone Service: Ready for the 21st Century?," Institute for Information Studies, 1991.

When the Northwest Electronic Campus was first conceived it was established that the needs of students would come first. Three original goals were agreed upon which have been met or exceeded: (1) to help students develop skill in accessing and utilizing on- and off-campus databases; (2) to facilitate communications between and among students, faculty and support staff; and (3) to enrich the academic environment on campus, particularly in the area of writing. Beyond accomplishing those goals, several serendipitous outcomes have been observed: enrollment has gone up 26 percent; the percentage of students wanting to move out of residence halls has dropped 50 percent so that now housing is fully utilized; and the overall image of the institution has been significantly enhanced as reported by school superintendents, principals and guidance counselors.

Finally, the Electronic Campus has been relatively easy to maintain and upgrade. It provides adequate electronic utilities so that students can develop proficiencies in their use and become prepared for the most modern working and learning environments. Northwest's Electronic Campus represents a viable, comprehensive, and low-cost model for the providing of electronic utilities which is a major challenge confronting post-secondary institutions today.

APPENDIX

Four

Appendix A: Campus Map

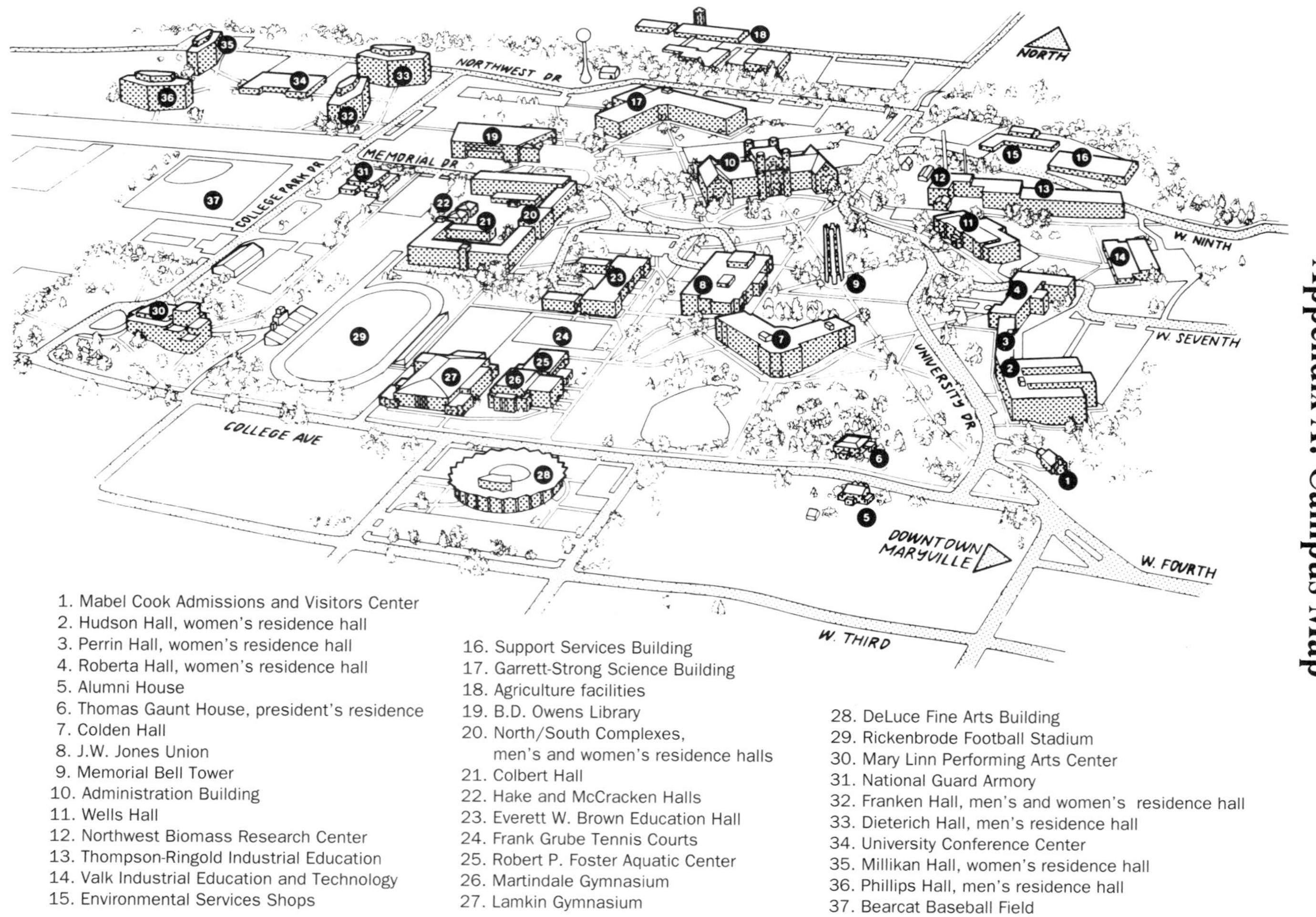

Appendix B: Northwest Electronic Campus Timeline

January 1978	PDP 11/70 with Gold Key word processing installed
June 1978	NSF grant for pre-college summer computing camps
July 1979	Computer moved from burned Administration Building
June 1980	VAX 11/780 with Gold Key word processing installed
August 1980	DECnet and MICOM 600 Data PBX installed
May 1981	DataMain on-line file manager written on VAX
July 1982	Residence halls and classroom buildings wired for cable TV
July 1982	Started installing over 400 microcomputers
October 1982	INFO retrieval system written and installed on VAX
March 1983	Computing Committee sets user station standards
November 1983	$25,000 library automation grant received
February 1984	Data PBX upgraded to multiple bay MICOM 6000
March 1984	Touch screen graphics information system created
October 1984	Touch Tone Telephone INFO written on VAX
May 1985	VAX 785 and 6 VAXstations on fiber Ethernet
June 1986	$1,180,000 Missouri appropriations started
July 1986	$1,200,000 auxiliary services loan approved
September 1986	VAX 8650 and clustering hardware installed
October 1986	Campus-wide exterior conduit system installed
December 1986	MICOM 6600 Data PBX added to the Instanet network
May 1987	TEXT retrieval system written and installed on VAX
June 1987	Terminals in every residence hall room and faculty office
July 1987	VAX instructional videodisc feed to cable TV
August 1987	Gov. John Ashcroft opens Electronic Campus for Class of 1991
January 1988	$89,000 DEC VAXstation 2000 grant received
June 1988	1,726,120 user sessions recorded first year
May 1989	Telephone service to every residence hall room
June 1989	2,634,455 user sessions recorded second year
August 1989	VAX Triple 8650 and Dual 785 cluster completed
December 1989	Disk caching software installed on VAX cluster
January 1990	VAX 8600 added to cluster for administration
March 1990	Library automation upgraded to ATLAS on VAX cluster
May 1990	3,312,973 user sessions recorded third year
June 1990	Using Computers class required for undergraduates
July 1990	LAN upgraded with fiber hub and thinwire to PC386s
November 1990	Telephone voice messaging services installed
December 1990	Video retrieval system upgraded to 72 disc jukebox
April 1991	Connection to MOREnet and other Wide Area Networks
May 1991	Voice messaging for every residence hall student and faculty member
May 1991	3,739,834 user sessions recorded fourth year
May 1991	Gov. Ashcroft "graduates" with Class of 1991

Appendix C: Electronic Campus Student Service Contract

COMPUTING SERVICE AGREEMENT NORTHWEST MISSOURI STATE UNIVERSITY

Terms and Conditions - Node 0 Computer Username Usage

Through this agreement, the Student accepts full responsibility for all charges incurred for printing initiated from his/her computer username account and any other charges associated with requested optional computing services provided by the institution. The Student acknowledges that it will be his/her responsibility to keep his/her password confidential and to immediately report any problems (including loss of the username password or unauthorized use of his/her computer username account) to the Computing Services Department.

Bills for printing and other optional services will be distributed, on a schedule set by the cashiering office, directly to the Student. Payment, in full, is required by the due date indicated. Upon notice from cashiering office that the Student is delinquent in payment, service will be discontinued without further notice. Service will not be restored until outstanding balances are rectified and payment has been posted. Nonpayment of services charges will be treated in the same manner as any other student debt. Withholding treasurer's approval for registration, diplomas, or transcripts may occur.

The Computing Services Department reserves the right to discontinue/deny service without notice to any Student it determines is abusing the computing system. Abuse includes, but is not limited to; physical damage to equipment, harassment to other users, wasting computing resources, and use of unauthorized usernames or passwords, bypassing accounting mechanisms, intentional disruption of the computer system by the launching of computer viruses, copying or duplicating software without authorization from the copyright holder, or duplication of system data files or programs equivalent to the system services.

USING UNAUTHORIZED USERNAMES FOR COMPUTING OR PRINTING IS THEFT OF SERVICE. ANY ATTEMPTS TO DEFRAUD THE INSTITUTION WILL BE REPORTED TO THE DEAN OF STUDENTS AND APPROPRIATE DISCIPLINARY ACTIONS WILL BE TAKEN.

Repair service requests which require dispatching of repair service personnel to the dormitory/residence and which result in no problem being found in the Computing Services Department's equipment or lines will result in a Repair Service charge. Maintenance of computer terminal, cable, wire and jacks other than that required from normal wear and use will result in a charge.

By signature on the COMPUTING SERVICE AGREEMENT FORM, the Student agrees to the terms and conditions stated above, and has read, understands, and accepts the charges described in, SUBSCRIBER RATES FOR COMPUTER USE. The Student will receive, at no charge, one authorized Node 0 computer username, password and one copy of the Computing Services Department's *User's Guide*, including Policies and Procedures.

Appendix D: Current Electronic Campus Data Network

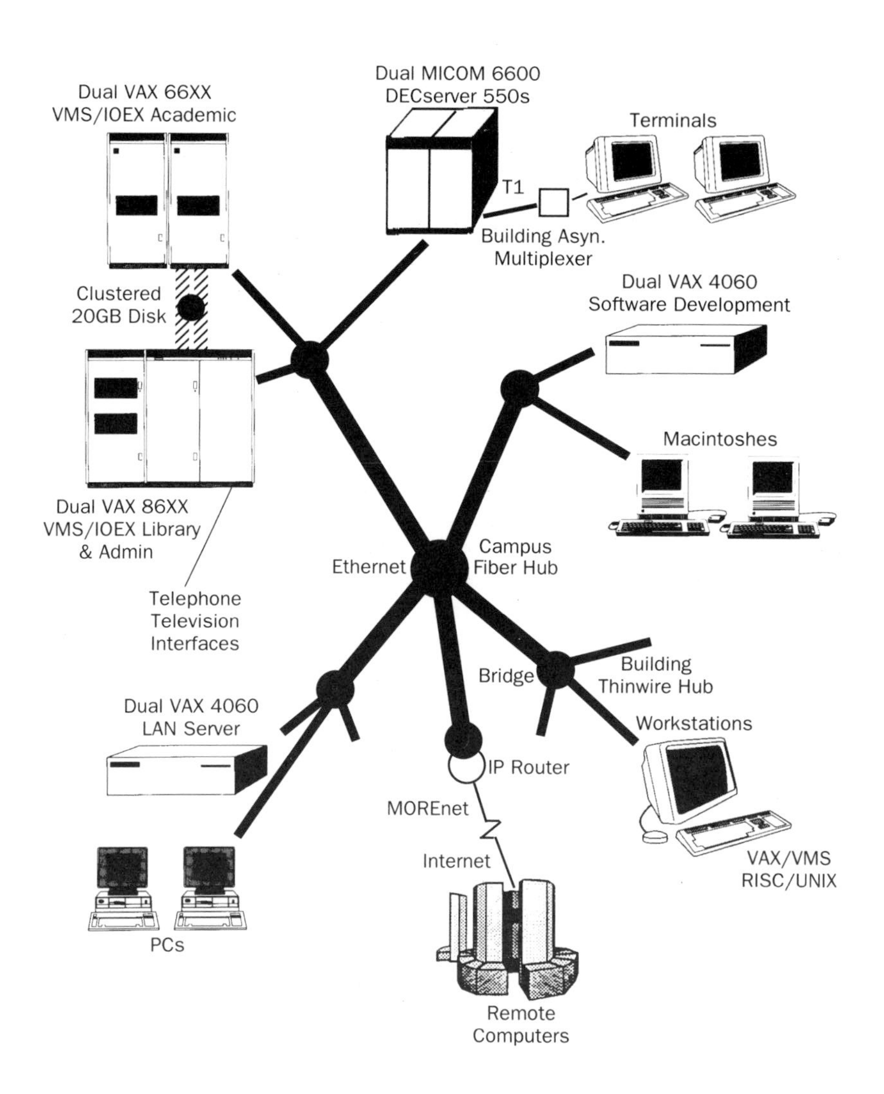

Appendix E: List of Figures

INDEX

JON T. RICKMAN

Dr. Rickman was born in Maryville, Missouri, where his grandfather Todd owned the Hanamo Telephone Company, and his parents graduated from Northwest Missouri State Teachers College. Dr. Rickman and his wife, Donna, have two daughters and one son.

Dr. Rickman completed his first computer programming course in 1962. After completing a Bachelor's and Master's Degree in Physics from Central Missouri State University, he worked in management for Southwestern Bell Telephone Company in St. Louis, Missouri.

Dr. Rickman completed his Ph.D. Degree in Computer Science from Washington State University in 1972 and taught Computer Science at The Pennsylvania State University in State College. He also consulted for the Vanda Corporation in New York City. He has been a member and actively involved in the Association for Computing Machinery since 1968.

Dr. Rickman returned to Maryville as a Professor in Computer Science and became Director of Computing Services at Northwest Missouri State University in 1977. He directed Computing Services starting with a single keyboard for interactive computing and a patch board for long distance telephone services. He has reported to three presidents at Northwest: Dr. Robert Foster, Dr. B.D. Owens and Dr. Dean Hubbard, who have all been advocates of strong computing and telecommunications services in higher education.

Dr. Rickman guided the electronic utilities at Northwest to their current nationally-recognized status with a staff of only 15 full-time people. He has always taken a personal interest in each software development project and has been actively involved with hardware and software system design work for nearly 30 years.

Dr. Rickman has served as the first Chair of the Governing Board of MOREnet, the Missouri Research and Education Network. Now in his second term as Chair, he continues to direct computing services, telecommunications, cable television and compressed video at Northwest.

His strong interest in information networks started at Washington State University under Dr. Bill Walden, where he helped design the SOLAR on-line abstract retrieval system. Dr. Rickman has authored over 30 papers and articles. His interest in computing power for computing networks started by authoring a chapter about planning computing power in *Administrative Computing in Higher Education,* 1979.

DEAN L. HUBBARD

Dr. Dean L. Hubbard is in his ninth year as president of Northwest Missouri State University, a position he assumed on August 1, 1984. Prior to coming to Northwest, he served as president of Union College, an independent liberal arts college in Lincoln, Nebraska.

Dr. Hubbard earned degrees from Stanford University (Ph.D.); Yonsei University, Seoul, Korea (Korean Language); and Andrews University, Berrien Springs, Michigan (B.A. and M.A.). He was born June 17, 1939, in Nyssa, Oregon. He and his wife, Aleta, have three grown children.

Dr. Hubbard's involvement with computers began while he was a graduate student at Stanford working on computer simulation models. During that time he received an EXXON Education Foundation grant to adapt such models to small colleges and universities. Later, he served on the National Center for Higher Education Management System's (NCHEMS) Institutional Data Uses Task Force, a group charged with analyzing the way data is used in higher education decision making. While president of Union College he led the first attempt to network computer terminals located in each student room and faculty office.

Under Dr. Hubbard's leadership, Northwest has received national attention for the 42 goals in its "Culture of Quality" plan to improve the quality of undergraduate education. In addition to the Electronic Campus, this plan encompasses the adoption of a clear set of competencies that every graduate must achieve, a comprehensive assessment program employing multiple measures of student attitudes and performance, a general education core, supplemental instruction in key courses, an advanced standing requirement, a program to focus upper division instruction and testing on higher order cognitive and affective skills, a writing across the curriculum program, integrative senior seminars, a faculty development program, and an undergraduate research program.

Dr. Hubbard has been a commissioner and is currently a consultant/evaluator for the North Central Association of Colleges and Schools. He has evaluated 23 colleges and universities for accreditation on three continents, and he has consulted to 29 hospitals, eight insurance companies, two denominations, and 12 colleges and universities. Included among the various organizations and commissions Dr. Hubbard has served are the Council on Public Higher Education in Missouri (president, 1988-89), the Missouri Governor's Advisory Council on Literacy (1987-88), the Committee on Literacy Skills for At-Risk Adults (chair, 1988-89), the American Association of State Colleges and Universities' committee on Excellence in Teaching and Learning (vice-chair), the American

Council on Education Advisory Committee on Campus Trends (current), and the National Summit on Mathematics Assessment (1991). In addition to 16 published articles, three book chapters, and numerous papers, Dr. Hubbard co-authored *The Quest for Quality: The Challenge for Undergraduate Education in the 1990's* (Jossey-Bass, 1990) and wrote the foreword to *Keeping the Promise: Improving the Quality of Undergraduate Education*, Patt VanDyke, ed., (the American Association of State Colleges and Universities, 1992).

Dr. Hubbard's international experience includes living in Seoul, Korea, for five years (1966-1971) and developing and consulting to language programs in six countries. In addition to extensive work in Asia, he has evaluated and consulted to educational institutions in Eastern and Western Europe and Central America.

ORDER FORM

The Electronic Campus

Name ______________________________

Mailing Address ______________________________

City ______________ State ______ Zip __________

The Electronic Campus – $14.95 x _____ copies = $_________

Add $3 per copy* for postage and handling $_________

Missouri residents add 5.725% sales tax $_________

Total enclosed $_________

Make check or money order payable to **Prescott Publishing** and mail along with this form to:

Prescott Publishing Co.
P.O. Box 713
Maryville, MO 64468

❑ Please charge my MasterCard account.

Card #______________________

Expiration Date ______________________

Credit card holders may order toll-free by calling 1-800-528-5197 or FAX orders to 816/562-1897

* Customers ordering 10 or more copies will not be charged shipping and handling.